THERE

IS

NO

OTHER

Swami Chetanananda

THERE

IS

NO

OTHER

RUDRA PRESS

PORTLAND, OREGON

Rudra Press
PO Box 13310
Portland, OR 97213-0310
phone/fax (503) 236-9878
www.rudrapress.com

Edited by Pat Tarzian
Cover photo and cover/book design by Lubosh Cech
Photo of the author by Barry Kaplan

Library of Congress Cataloging-in-Publication Data

Chetanananda, Swami, 1948-
    There is no other / Swami Chetanananda.
        p. cm.
    ISBN 0-915801-88-4
    1. Spiritual life. 2. Conduct of life. I. Title.

BL624.C4533 1999
294.5'44—dc21

                                    99-056811

Never are there two things....There is only one.

There is no "other."

What gets in the way of our experience of joy?
The simplest way to put it is — attachment.
As long as we think of ourselves as individual
people with individual issues and an
individualized struggle, we are taking infinite
spaciousness and infinite potentiality and
shrinking them down to a set of limited
circumstances. The fundamental reality of a
human being **is** *infinite space and vibrant*
potentiality. That is what we truly are.

~

Swami Chetanananda

Contents

About the Author *ix*

Editor's Note *xi*

What Do We Want to Do with the Rest of Our Life? *1*

Oneness *11*

Pain *17*

Do It for the Love *25*

Disappointment *29*

Compassion *33*

Mind *41*

Obstacles *45*

Karma *49*

Children and Relationships *55*

The Myth of Personal Control *61*

Why Are We Here? *69*

Attachment *75*

Doubt *85*

Trust the Process *95*

The Religion of the Law, the Spirituality of Love *105*

The Union of Power and Compassion *117*

Salvation *123*

Ritual and Purity: The Havan *131*

We Are Here to Burn *139*

Perfect Clarity *145*

Yoga *153*

Spiritual Practice Is Our Daily Life *161*

The Teacher and Our Own Humanity *173*

Alignment *185*

Consecrated Action *189*

Getting Over Ourselves to Give of Our Self *193*

The Basis of Spiritual Growth *201*

We Are An Energy Event *209*

Death of a Loved One *215*

Fear, Transcendence, and Heroes, Like Us *219*

Chöd: The Ritual Practice of Surrender and Self-Sacrifice *235*

A Life of Love *263*

About the Author

SWAMI CHETANANANDA, Swamiji, was born in the Midwest and educated at Indiana University. He studied with Swami Rudrananda in New York from 1971 to 1973, receiving the lineage mantle from him. In 1978, Swami Chetanananda was initiated into the Saraswati order of sannyasis at Ganeshpuri at the behest of Swami Muktananda. From 1980 to 1986, Swamiji had extensive contact with Swami Laksman Joo in Srinagar, studying Kashmir Shaivism. Swamiji has traveled widely, exploring the religious practices of many cultures.

As abbot of the Nityananda Institute and Rudrananda Ashram based in Portland, Oregon, Swami Chetanananda is developing a translation program for both Sanskrit and Tibetan texts. He has been initiated into the ancient Buddhist ritual practices of Phowa and Chöd. Swamiji has expertise in Indian, Tibetan, and Indonesian art, as well as in the history and archaeology of the Far East. He has studied, in depth, asana practice, cranial osteopathy, homeopathy, and acupuncture and is the author of several books, including *Dynamic Stillness*, *The Breath of God*, *Will I Be the Hero of My Own Life?* and *Choose To Be Happy*.

Editor's Note

⁓

THERE IS NO OTHER is composed of a series of talks given by Swami Chetanananda between August 1997 and December 1998. The talks were minimally edited, given titles, and then presented as chapters in this book. These chapters have not been arranged in chronological order but rather according to the flow of subject matter. The talks were prepared and given by Swami Chetanananda with this book in mind.

The reader may note that both the words "ourself" and "ourselves" are used in the book, sometimes in the same sentence. They refer to different, although not separate, entities. "Ourself" reflects the spiritual core that lies at the heart of all of us; "ourselves" refers to the more superficial parts of us. When Swami Chetanananda speaks, the words are used with these meanings, which have been preserved in the book.

There are several people who worked long hours to bring these talks to book form. Many thanks go to Sharon Ward, as reader of the final manuscript; to Lubosh Cech, for the cover and book design; to the transcribing team of Lisa Hoberg, Leiko Coyle, Connie Dyer, Vivina Boster, and Mira Ames; and to proofreader Karen Jones.

Pat Tarzian

WHAT DO WE WANT TO DO WITH THE REST OF OUR LIFE?

~

"The real goal of spiritual people is to become completely clear in the head and in the heart. And to become completely clear in our head and heart, we have to transcend all our agendas.... Our life is not about getting what we want. Our life is about giving what we can."

WHAT DO WE WANT TO DO WITH the rest of our life? What is *really* important to us? This is not an overly serious question: Life is about something wonderful, and all the spiritual work we do increases our joy and the flow within us and our capacity to share with others. But we do not have a long time here—none of us has a long time. This life is precious. The Buddhists say it is difficult and rare to attain a human body. Unlike other animals, we have an extraordinary opportunity: We are not entirely at the mercy of our environment; we have some choices; and while we suffer and die, feel stresses, strains, and pressures, we also have a sense that there is a deeper possibility of getting over the general struggle of this existence.

So we have one chance to do it right, and the time is now. What are we going to do with the rest of our life? We have only the present moment—the past is gone, the future is, well, future. What are we going to do with our life now?

Most people, however creative or energetic, end up bowing to the commercial values of the culture. They want to make a lot of money. They want to have a relationship. They want this and that. Acquisition is what they want to do with this life.

But if there is something precious about life, does it make sense that we are going to find that preciousness in anything we do not already have—in anything we have to struggle to get or to keep? If struggle were the essence of

~

life, life would not be special or precious at all. Joy and inner peace would be impossible, and pretty much anything we did would leave us constantly dissatisfied.

We may feel constantly dissatisfied, but that is not the essence of life; that is the nature of commerce. What is the nature of commerce? Desire. Give me more. That thought permeates much of religion as well: The whole idea of sin and heaven has to do with desire and our capacity to *earn* our way into a different state. But only when desire is finished may we achieve a complete and total union with God, and only that union puts an end to our individual strivings and strugglings, comings and goings, ups and downs, arounds and arounds.

If we want an end to struggle, that is the same as an end to desire, and so we take all desires and bundle them into one desire that is pointed at the highest—the desire to grow. We really have to want to grow. And the thing that accompanies that wish to grow is a mind that strives for perfection, for union with God, for perfect clarity.

When we talk about the desires of this world and freeing ourselves from desire, we are not talking about renunciation, which is not a liberation but a suppression.

Practitioners of ages past recognized that desire is a natural function of the manifestation of the power of spirit in the realm of diversity. They knew that desire has tremendous power to release, when focused appropriately, and to bind, when focused inappropriately—power to clarify when focused properly, to confuse when focused improperly. Practitioners of ancient times knew that desire is one of the fundamental powers that can support diversity or provide a pathway to its transcendence. The key is where desire is focused.

When we see clearly, when we discover the perfect clarity within ourself, we do not do what is unhealthy for us; we do not pursue things that do not have an ultimate higher end. In India, in poorer countries, renunciation plays an important role because people deny themselves for the sake of doing service for others, and that is productive. But there are many ways to make sacrifices. If we keep in mind our highest best interest as well as the highest best interest of the whole, then renunciation is not the focus; service, compassion, and love are. We find within ourself an authentic and enduring experience of love that we cultivate, and that love manifests in as many ways as

~

we walk about in this world. We are clear and express ourself simply, and love takes care of the rest.

All the practices we undertake should ground our minds in the contact with the specialness that is the source of mind. The mind itself comes from this specialness that is the fundamental quality of Life Itself. This union with God, this grounding of the mind in the source of all life, puts an end to struggle, to striving, to suffering. This is "bliss," although the term in no way addresses the multidimensional potentiality of that foundational state from which mind, body, and all things have coalesced. If we are not in this world attempting to stabilize ourselves in something higher and finer, then we are doomed to have as our only choice the game of life. And the game of life has one rule: If we play, we lose.

Many people end up abandoning their spiritual practice for the game of life, for the sake of some agenda, such as relationships or career accomplishments. The game of life is insidious. Artists who sell their work become conditioned to the marketplace; physicians who sell their service become conditioned to the marketplace; and every human being who has some desire becomes conditioned to the marketplace. And then everything a person does is about getting something.

This applies to relationships as well. We must think carefully—are we offering authentic love to the people with whom we share our life, or are we peddling an agenda? Are we about giving real love or getting something we think we have to have?

This reminds me of the cuttlefish, which changes its color to attract mates, repel predators, and entice food. Human beings are basically colonies of cells, just like the cuttlefish, and we know that we, too, consume lots of energy looking for opportunities to eat and reproduce. We may not like to think of ourselves this way, but the parallel is evident. So the question is: Is it lunch, or is it authentic love?

It is so important that we understand that every thing is impermanent—every thing. Every thing dies or disintegrates, and not even "I" exists, not really. "I" is a temporary condensation, a temporary aggregate of elements. When we break "I" down, it is just a colony of cells, like the cuttlefish. And all the things of this world are just different forms of cellular organization, different orders of

~~~

magnitude of sophistication that lead to biological entities.

In the Judeo-Christian culture, a human being is an individual soul created by God; that soul is at the core of the body—it is individual, separate. According to Judeo-Christian culture, God judges us based on the quality of our performance and then assigns us a position within the structure of the hierarchy of eternity. Yet many serious people throughout the ancient world, in Asia and in Europe, thought about this subject deeply and carefully, and nobody could find within themselves an individual soul. There is only one thing and that is Consciousness—a pure, subtle, refined Awareness that differentiates Itself first as space and motion and then as all appearances. But space and motion and all appearances are never separate from Consciousness, and the appearances that present themselves in the field of this unity of space and motion are all temporary. Only the process is infinite, only Consciousness is eternal.

Add to this our knowledge of modern-day biology—we are all just colonies of cells—and we see more clearly. There is no thing to cling to, and in fact there is no one really to do the clinging. There is just temporary condensation upon condensation with a temporary set of characteristics we call "identity." But none of it is real; none of it is permanent. Or perhaps I should say, it is real the way a dream is real. We have the experience of a dream, things happen in a dream, but a dream comes and goes and is replaced by other dreams. There is nothing to hold onto—no thing.

Never are there two things—not ever. There is only one. There is no "other." From the highest perspective, bondage and liberation have the same source; heaven and hell, nirvana and samsara all have the same source. They are not the same things, but everything has the same source. No thing is eternal, no concept, no construct. There is no eternal heaven and no eternal hell; there are only states. What is permanent is change, what is eternal is process. Suffering arises from our ignorance of this fact. The Buddhists call it "ego-clinging," the Hindus call it "attachment," but whatever it is called, its source is desire and its effect is struggle.

Sometimes when we have an itch, it feels good to scratch it. For a moment. But then we scratch and scratch and create a sore, and the itch does not stop anyway. So we have to take care of the sore. And the antibiotics we take for the sore cause some other condition, and we have to take care of that, and so on and on. Desire is like that. We scratch that itch, and then we are stuck in a cycle where there is no amount of scratching or tending that is going to fix the issue.

There is no other enemy we have, no other threat in our life, except for ego-clinging, attachment. Seeing this, we understand that human beings struggle with impermanence and desire and suffer terribly. Most are on a treadmill with just enough positive feedback to keep them going but not enough to stop them from being hungry. Many human beings are in tremendous pain, suffering perpetually, and so we have some genuine compassion for everyone. We transcend the discussion of, "This is a bad person, that is a good person." There may be a lot of ignorant, unclear, insatiably desirous people who are suffering, but that does not make them bad. Understanding this gives us a real willingness to serve *all* humanity. We do not think, "This one is deserving, that one is not."

The real goal of spiritual people is to become completely clear in the head and in the heart. And to become completely clear in our head and heart, we have to transcend all our agendas. The more the power of spirit expands in us through our practice, the more clarity comes to us. Confusion ceases and the dissatisfaction that keeps us constantly churning up a new desire dissolves. We burn up our concerns, struggles, issues—our selves—and we become liberated like that.

In perfect clarity, the infinite potential that is present in Life Itself manifests in and through us as divine love. Then what the rest of our life is about is establishing ourself in a state beyond agendas and desires, in a place where we serve humanity as a manifestation of that divine love. We hold to the power of love inside us, and our life transforms itself, not into what we want but into what it wants for us. And this is infinitely better than anything we can come up with, because our imaginations are not so great as Life's capacity to provide.

Perfect clarity is the goal, and the hallmarks of that clarity are humility and compassion. And this is the final and ultimate, absolutely true secret teaching, and that is: We have to sacrifice. Our life is not about getting what we want. Our life is about giving what we can.

ONENESS

~~~

"The truth is, the meaning of life is whatever meaning we

uncover from the infinite spaciousness, the vibrant potentiality,

the oneness that is our source; and the quality of our life

experience depends upon that meaning."

Someone recently said to me that they have never had the experience of oneness. It is important to understand that everyone is always having the experience of oneness. Everyone. It is there; there is no other; there is only one. All appearance of other is nothing more than the vitality of the One manifesting Itself. Everything has the same source. Our belief in diversity is nothing more than what we choose to focus on. Oneness is there—and it is the true nature of Life Itself—but we may be too busy trying to do something or get something to feel it. I promise you, if it is not there, then neither are we.

Practice is essential to our continuous awareness of oneness. I am constantly searching texts and meeting people to see different ways of practice, different ways to view and express our physical mechanism and the range of capabilities intrinsic to our nervous and psychic systems. And all any of this is about is the experience of oneness. When we approach our daily life with concentration and an awareness of the power of our own creative ability, we find a rhythm within ourself and a flow in our daily life that facilitate change in us. Working the same way year after year is fine, but it is not going to get us to every depth, breadth, and height of the contact with the creative potential within us.

The ultimate experience, the absolute complete enlightenment, is already present in us. But we cannot hang back from it like mice. We have to be like lions and tigers about it; we go for it, roar for it. When we have a wish to grow, we don't squeak it: "Oh, please, would it be at all possible, do you think maybe just a tiny bit, if it's not too much bother, may I grow?" We roar it; we mean it; we believe in

~

our Self. Life is special, our opportunity, extraordinary. This is a precious thing; we take hold of it.

We have a wonderful chance; we *can* believe in it, and in believing in it, we learn to believe in our Self deeply. We learn to find in ourself our source, which is profoundly powerful and empty at the same moment. Then we live from that powerful emptiness that is completely full, that is the oneness everywhere and in us at once. From within us, we release all tensions, all struggle, and become liberated from our personal history, finding within ourself continuously a new Life that is sweet. This power, this oneness, does not make us a big shot; it does not make us important. It makes us more nothing than we were before—and with such love and sweetness that we see there is nothing more to want. With this love and sweetness, everything becomes possible.

We do not have any problem; what we have is work to do, which is a joy. We do the work, and we do it with love, together; we have fun doing it because we make it fun. We care about each other, and in the process of working together and caring about each other, we learn to communicate in new ways. We cultivate within ourself and show in our environment the richness that is our contact with that profound, highest spiritual potential within us. We show how powerful and wonderful that can be.

So we need not have any doubt—we have had the experience of oneness—it is there. And through our practice, our mindfulness, as we move through each day, we learn more about the reach and range of our creative capacity. We learn how our careful words and careful touch, our careful feelings for our environment and the people in it, are of benefit to everyone, awakening within us an understanding of the direct experience of the mind of God, which is at the core of our existence.

We are not limited, struggling, squeaky-voiced, scared creatures. We absolutely are not that. Oneness is the ground of all experience; complete creative potential is within us; contact with the power of spirit within us is always available to us. And perseverance in this process is everything. If we really want to grow, we cannot give up. Some days, it will be wonderful and exciting, and we will run to it with exuberance. Other days, we may have to drag ourselves to it. But perseverance is everything—persevering with devotion and love.

~

This process is going to take us places we never imagined we would go and expose us to experiences and feelings we did not imagine existed. Sometimes the response to that is to suppress or repress or just plain to want to run away. Sometimes we will journey through unknown territory, taking on tasks the purpose of which is not entirely clear until done—and maybe not even then—and sometimes taking on tasks that seem impossible to accomplish. But because they are tasks that are in front of us, they are part of our life process, and we do them with devotion and love.

There is one rule that all authentic practitioners have lived by for centuries and still live by, and that one rule is: Don't hold back. The truth is, the meaning of life is whatever meaning we uncover from the infinite spaciousness, the vibrant potentiality, the oneness that is our source; and the quality of our life experience depends upon that meaning. The devotion and love we constantly dig up from within ourself allow our life to have a meaning that is the richness that oneness truly is. When we persevere with devotion and love, roar with devotion and love from our deepest capacity, we benefit the All that is the One.

PAIN

❦

"Every state we can discuss is oneness. Even pain."

*H*INDUS BELIEVE THAT SUFFERING arises because of ignorance, the Buddhists, because of ego-clinging. But whether the cause is called ignorance or ego-clinging, the meaning is the same: Emotional pain occurs because of our holding onto conditioning and because of our entanglement in chemistry. That chemistry is real and palpable; it has power, energy, the capacity to influence our behavior. But unlike many other biological entities, human beings have the ability to make choices. We have the potential to see through the biochemical clouds floating around us, through the external stimuli that constantly call us to opportunities for getting this or that, which may not be in our highest interest. We have the possibility of seeing the results of our actions and of making an assessment of the effect of those results on our life. And we can choose.

~

Our suffering and struggling are real pain, but they are not necessary. They arise because of our attachment to a misunderstanding we have about our nature and our function. We may think that our function is to accumulate territory in order to secure a position. This applies to relationships, careers, to most of our worldly concerns. But this is not our deepest nature, our authentic function. The core of our biological existence is the same as the core of our spiritual one—it is the creative power that lies within each of us. The antidote to pain is to reach into ourself every single day to find the rhythm, the flow of that creative power, and to allow that creative power continually to refine and re-express itself in the field of our activity.

Our main concern needs to be how endlessly to refine ourself and serve our entire environment—how to generate a flow within ourself that uplifts us and everyone around us. More and more as this refinement takes place, the expansion of the creative power within us becomes so great that our physical body and the patterns of tension that completely absorb all this energy are dissolved. Then the power of spirit manifests itself in different and palpable dimensions throughout our life. A simple way to put this

~

is: We begin to experience the power of love at work in our life instead of the problem of pain.

In order to serve our environment—which is what our inner refinement seeks to do because the power of love *is* service—we have to see clearly the impermanence of the entity we call "me" or "I." Our physical equipment is not designed to last long. God seems to be more of an artist than an engineer. Add to this the fact that the core of individuality we think we are does not exist. The same creative power that is in me is in you and the person next to you and the person down the road from you and the people you do not even know. Never is there anything but one thing. Never. There is only the power of spirit manifesting everywhere. There is no other.

Even our work is not "our" work. When we think about doing "our" work, we are reinforcing within ourselves the egotism, separateness, and disintegration that impede the appropriate understanding of what it is we are attempting to accomplish. This separateness, egotism, and disintegration are the foundation of pain. Every one of us has work to do, but it is not "our" work because all of us have the same work to do. It is *the* work of connecting to and cultivating our awareness of the power of spirit, allowing it to expand so that we see that "our" work is not what we are doing—it is the growing of that power that we are about, the growing of that power for the benefit of everyone and everything in our life.

In Buddhism, there is something called the Bodhisattva vow. Bodhisattvas are beings who are completely enlightened but who are willing to take rebirth again and again in order to help mankind. The vow means that Bodhisattvas wait until everybody is enlightened before they enjoy the fruits of their own enlightenment, such as no more rebirth. The Bodhisattva vow means that we feel compassion for all human beings, and so the work is never individual because the work each one of us does is to benefit every one of us. But the meaning of the vow goes even beyond this: Through the Bodhisattva vow, we are awakening within ourself and allowing to express through the whole of our existence a living, dynamic field of transformation.

So our work is not our own individual work. Instead of reinforcing this misunderstanding, which in turn reinforces old patterns of scars, thickness, and walls, we dissolve all

~

that. The truth is, we do not even do *the* work. It is the creative power within us that does everything. What we can do is to choose that creative power over all misunderstanding, and embrace and reinforce that power. Then we see the total unity of space and motion. We see in the one, the whole and in the whole, the one. One in the many, the many in one.

The simplest articulation of that creative power is our breath. When we are having a sense that in some way we are not in contact with that oneness, let us watch our breath. Stop. Stop thinking. Stop fighting. Stop struggling. Even when we are in pain—especially when we are in pain—watch the breath. Feel the muscles relax. Feel that.

Every state we can discuss is oneness. Even pain. The only thing troublesome about pain is that it reinforces behavior that reinforces the sense of alienation and separateness that reinforces the pain and suffering, and we have a self-reinforcing system that we are trying to see through. We must see through it in order to release a higher order of potentiality present within us, and that is an infinitely more satisfying place from which to participate in life.

So we are not trying to suppress pain; we are not even

saying it is a bad thing. We are saying that a sense of alienation causes us health problems, on every level, that are unnecessary. When we see to the core of our existence, alienation has nothing to do with the power that is there.

A deeper order of integration requires some surrender of individuality, in a social, or interpersonal, and biochemical sense. Resistance may come up, and it is painful; this is work, and it takes energy to release energy. But there is no loss of energy in the process, only the expansion of energy, because the energy we apply and the energy we release become a part of our potential.

We have to practice and connect to a deeper place within ourself and then be unattached to the circumstances in which we find ourself—and that is always. We must understand that our lives change, and change is a good thing. Within the circumstances in which we exist, there is constantly motion—there is a drawing close and a coming apart, a coming close and a drawing apart. Rather than trying to make something happen over here, generating this or that in order to have a specific material goal, we forget our external attachments and have solely and completely the deepest commitment to growing. Then the circumstances around us will sort themselves out. If we change our field of focus from what we imagine to be a problem to the potential for transformation, the pain may not go away, but it does not dominate our awareness anymore. It does not control our choice-making process.

Human beings may have lots of problems, but the creative potential, the spirit, that is the source of our existence has no problem. It has only infinite potentiality and profound fullness. That is what we want to connect to because everything we think of as a problem now will die with us—everything. But that source, that power, lives on and is completely beyond pain and death. The human condition is one in which we are bound to feel some pain. Change and uncertainty, which are the core of all, are a bit painful. But when we live our life in contact with the finest part of us, we stop struggling. Problems no longer command us. We are established in a state of clarity that allows us to treat everyone, including ourselves, with kindness and compassion. Then the possibility of not participating in the brutalities of this world is enhanced.

We have to learn to trust even the painful feelings that arise in us. We have to trust the uncertainty, so that endlessly we are allowing the creative power, which in its essence is total uncertainty, to manifest and bring us total benefit. We have to be careful and subtle when we think about what "total benefit" means; all benefit is not warm and fuzzy. Wrathful deities are a way in Buddhism and Hinduism to say that beneficial is not always warm and fuzzy. If we think warm and fuzzy, we will misunderstand and miss many opportunities.

So we cultivate the wisdom within ourself. We do not continue to misunderstand our true nature but instead refine our understanding and in so doing, extend it to bring ourself continuously to a higher, more powerful, and palpable experience of joy and satisfaction in our participation in Life. The more we fight, struggle, and perpetuate self-reinforcing patterns of tension, pain, and prejudice, the more we deny the possibility of living in the most satisfying, wonderful, beneficial-to-everybody-we-know dimension of existence. This dimension, which is beyond suffering, is what is valuable in our life.

DO IT FOR THE LOVE

"We do what we do every day with love and devotion....not because we are trying to please anyone we think is judging us.... We do it for the love because that is the kind of person we want to be—that is the kind of person we are."

WHATEVER WE DO, WE SHOULD do it for the love of it. Doing things with and for love is valuable, and this is whether or not we are earning something for the work we do. Whatever we do with love enriches our life. In our daily work, when we make a good product, we make something that truly serves somebody, and we do it for the love of the whole process. When we do not do it for the love, if something does not go the way we planned, we may feel broken, a failure. This is not the case when we do what we do with love.

~

So if we are to earn a living and we are not at the point where we can make money doing what we love, then we wait tables, change oil, pump gas, sweep the floor, do whatever, with love. And we recognize that this is the beginning of investing in what we really love to do. This is how we build an authentic life. And we do not give up.

Real love manifests most powerfully in perseverance. We keep going, we keep working at it. So much of the challenge in our life is the highest creative power within us manifesting itself as some difficulty and teaching us about ourself and itself and about the extraordinary potentiality that exists within. Hardship is not about what a bad person we are or what a bad person someone else is. It is about each of us deciding exactly what kind of person we are going to be.

We do what we do every day with love and devotion. We try to have expansive lives full of love and respect for everybody, not because we are trying to please anyone we think is judging us and not because we are worried about what God is going to feel about us when this is all over. We do it for the love because that is the kind of person we want to be—that is the kind of person we are.

The truly important moments in our life, the important experiences, do not give us a second chance. The most important moments, we have one chance at, and that is it. We practice every single second of every single day because we do not know which day, which hour, will bring that pivotal moment. And if we are always doing what we are doing with love and respect, then when those precious moments arise, we will appreciate the preciousness in them, and one chance will be enough.

DISAPPOINTMENT

"Disappointment comes when we think the experience of the infinite can be found in a book or in...entertainment.... In any thing. When we insist on relating an experience of contact with the sublime to some object...we are insulting our soul and denying ourself...the value...ever present within us."

W HAT SEPARATES US FROM ONE another and keeps us in the orbit of life into which we were born is the weight of accumulated disappointment. The power of spirit lies underneath the tensions of the accumulated disappointment of ordinary living. In every person, underneath the disappointment, there is something pure and powerful. In its contracted form, it is desire; in

⁓

its expanded form, it is love. Kundalini is the connection between the two—the process of unfoldment of that contracted power of desire into love.

There really is no issue of "problem"; there is disappointment, which builds condensation, crystallization. Penetrated by the power of our wish to grow, that crystallization shatters, and the unfoldment that takes place from within changes our understanding of what we are. We are not a thing, we are a process, and the boundaries of that process are infinite. There is a place in each of us to which the wish to grow can penetrate, a place where we are still authentic, pure, untouched by the disappointment that has landed on us. Because of our contact with that place beyond disappointment, a resonance emerges.

The experience of the infinite is sublime. Each one of us has had, if just for a moment, an experience of that infinite. Disappointment comes when we think the experience of the infinite can be found in a book or in some form of entertainment, in eating a great hot dog or drinking a can of beer. In any thing. When we insist on relating an experience of contact with the sublime to some object—relationships included—we are insulting our soul and denying ourself value—the value that is ever present within us. Then disappointment is the result.

When we follow our breath, we are able to reach through the tension of accumulated disappointment to the true experience of the infinite, which is the power of spirit within. That power absolutely is there. We have a choice: to focus on desire, which can lead only to disappointment in the quality of what we do get or in the notion of what we have not gotten—or to focus on the essence of who and what we are, which is the power that created the whole universe. That power has nothing to do with disappointment. To the contrary. That power is complete fulfillment, ever and always.

COMPASSION

"...compassion and devotion...are simply the most powerful things in the world."

COMPASSION PROVIDES THE environment in which we can rise above the turmoil, brutality, confusion, and struggle of the mundane aspects of our existence. Too often people deal with hard times by being intolerant of one another: Everybody is against something. Ultimately, we have to forget about being against anything and be *for* something, which is love and respect for Life.

A compassionate person does not spend their time thinking too much. A compassionate person just keeps their heart open and tries to love and respect all people all the time. Life is hard for everybody; everybody has to face the maximum injustice in this world. When we understand that the corollary to the statement, "*That* jerk!" is,

"This jerk!" then we see that the compassionate corollary to both is: Compassion for ourself means compassion towards others.

To demonstrate compassion, it helps if we have communication skills and learn to talk nicely to people without suppressing what we have to say. It also helps if we learn to listen, hearing what people say without getting caught up in their issues or ours—in fact, without having any issues in which to get caught up. It may be that the intensity of our spiritual practice causes us to have a fire inside that rattles our eardrums. The intensity of the process may mean that words come out stronger than we had intended. So we say, "I'm sorry," and try again. But "I'm sorry" only works so many times. Then our credibility is shot. So we try to watch the flow of communication without getting tangled up as we watch. We focus on our breath, on the flow, and after that, we learn to trust the process.

Being a compassionate person is not about being right; it is about growing, being transformed, learning to love, developing the ability to appreciate the profound power of devotion. So few people understand what compassion and devotion truly are; they are simply the most powerful

~

things in the world. We can experience a transformation through our spiritual practice which will awaken a profound power in us and allow that power to flow in ways that transform the total landscape of our life. This power brings us, and as many human beings as possible, peace, prosperity, and deep understanding. Devotion brings us to this power; compassion is the result of it.

Life is a paradox; it is everything at once. We cannot address this paradox with our minds. We can be aware of it in our minds, but we have to cultivate through our practice a contact with an authentic place in us, and from that authentic place, we can relate to and feel this paradox. In feeling it, in attuning our nerves, muscles, veins to this paradox, we become interconnected with it to a degree that the paradox is resolving itself on a moment by moment basis in the field of our awareness. Then we are capable of loving everyone, capable of true compassion.

In this state of total interconnectedness, where is the "bad" experience? Who, in a state of expansion, has bad experiences? As the paradox of life continuously rearranges itself, we have challenging experiences. But these are change, growth, expansion in our lives. These are not bad experiences.

People who authentically practice to understand life and to grow as human beings are able to take life in whole, with all its tensions, pain, confusion, paradox. Through our authentic and completely sincere endeavor, we attune ourself to the paradox of life to the degree that we appreciate the extraordinary harmony and beauty underlying the dynamism.

One of the most important things about my experience with my teacher, Rudi, Swami Rudrananda, was the paradox of his being and not being at the same time—the paradox of his being a completely "human" being and at the same time, a being of unimaginable magic in his soul. That magic operated for the benefit of other human beings at great expense to himself. He was deeply compassionate; he was completely open. He was never about what it looked like—in himself or anyone else.

Because of the interconnectedness of everything, if we cannot open our hearts to and appreciate the paradox operating in each person, what we are actually doing is suppressing and denying ourself—because of fear, because of tension. Compassion begins with compassion for ourself. And compassion is not an endpoint in itself; it is part of

~

our spiritual practice; it is opening our hearts. We do not say, "Let's open our hearts to the things we like, while choking, judging, and complaining about everything else." We say, "Let's open our hearts and find a flow every day." We do not say, "...when we feel like it;" we say, "We keep our hearts open every single day, whether we make money or not, whether our relationships work out or not."

Rather than criticizing human beings as they struggle, we open our hearts and extend our energy to them, allowing them in their own time to resolve their situation in a beneficial fashion. We keep our hearts open when we look at difficult human interactions; our minds are completely quiet. Free from worldly tensions, we contemplate the paradox of life, the paradox of our existence and nonexistence at the same time. We recognize the dreamlike quality that is our everyday and every-way experience. I say "dreamlike" because life is like a dream—it is real and not real at the same moment. Because it is forever changing, forever transforming itself and us—as well as eventually putting an end to our physical existence—life has a certain unreality to it. Because we are here at this moment, doing, feeling, life has substantiality to it as well.

~

In appreciating this paradox, there is a step beyond, and that is commitment. If we are not committed to growing, then as we start to practice, and as the tensions, poisons, and basic limitations—genetic and otherwise, with which we have come into this life—start to release, the tendency will be to resuppress them. If we are not able continually to come back to our practice and to a compassion for ourself and others, then we will clamp down on the release, and our system will turn on itself, consuming itself.

So instead of rules and regulations, we have a compassion that is the touchstone, the loving place within ourself where we can always come. We know there is a perfectly simple, clear place that, if we choose to sit down and be in contact with it, will bring us to a state of total well-being, whatever our momentary physical or external condition. Living in contact with simple clarity, we are compassionate and loving human beings who recognize that all the tensions, pressures, and issues we get twisted around have no reality whatsoever. Recognizing that nonreality, we breathe into and feel the expansion of the creative power within us—we feel a sense of complete well-being—and we recognize that power as Awareness Itself.

~

Our individual practice operates to its fullest potential in an environment of compassion, which allows our practice to become increasingly refined and to operate in a transpersonal dimension. In this way, we come directly to participate in the whole of Life. We do not think about it; we feel it. Every time the brain takes over, we shift awareness to the breath, and feel and feel.

Spiritual work is not about thinking; it is about feeling our vitality in all forms and feeling those forms authentically. Tuning into vitality, we follow it back to its source, to the power of spirit. And this we can only do in an internal environment of openness and an experiential environment of compassion, which we understand to be, ultimately, one and the same.

MIND

❧

"When people talk with and from love, what mind is there in that?"

*T*HE POWER OF SPIRIT THAT IS
pure potentiality and ultimate reality is not readily understood because of mind. Some practitioners in ancient times
referred to the source of life as a kind of grand mind, but the
mind that plans our daily activities and churns our desires is
not that Mind. The mind of our daily activities tricks us
into thinking that the appearance of diversity in everyday
living is what is important in Life.

The mind, when left to its own devices, scrambles everything and forgets about it immediately. Our intellect, a part
of us deeper than mind, may appreciate interactions we have
with people, but ultimately it is our mind that determines
how the information of any interaction is structured—what
transformative effect it might or might not have.

~

The mind is not very important, except in its unproductive qualities: It is the repository of fear, the source of tensions. It is how we think about things, and thinking is what creates tensions. When we find what is deeper in us and live from that dimension, our mind is transformed into a vehicle for supporting and sustaining our endeavor.

If we were to become highly creative painters, we could not be overly concerned with making money and remain true artists for long; yet our minds might constantly tell us: "We need to make money. We need this and that." So if we are to be creative first and foremost, we cannot listen to that part of ourselves that keeps score. We have to listen to something deeper.

In the same way, we do not understand our spiritual practice from our minds. Anybody listening in their heads will not truly hear or productively process one word that is said regarding spiritual work. Only when we calm our minds, truly calm them, do we have the possibility of appreciating a much bigger universe. The mind plays no real role in spiritual work: Through it, we hear an instruction and try to apply it; but for the work to have meaning, there has to be a bell rung deeper in us. Otherwise, there is

~

no follow-through, no power to act on the sharing that has taken place.

The more we think about anything, the less we do it. The mind is for people who talk about art, not for people who make it. That is an essential distinction. All art—musical, pictorial, whatever—comes from a place that has no mind. The minute art hits the place where it has a mind, it is not art anymore—it is business. The same is true of spiritual work.

When people talk with and from love, what mind is there in that? When people speak from true passion about Life, what mind is there in that? When we are truly alive to our Life, what mind is there in that?

There is no mind that can encompass the passion of Life, the intensity of authentic love, and when that passion, that intensity, rises up in us to the highest place it can go, that is khecari mudra. That is when our individuality is totally burned up in the fire of love, and we are in the cool joy of infinite space, recognizing that every word, feeling, and impulse we have are not from our physical body but are extensions of pure potentiality. We see that our feelings, thoughts, work, direction, and inspiration are not just from our present daily life. Dwelling in all of us are the currents of different lifetimes, hitting one another and creating resonance, and in these crosscurrents, the power of love and creativity expresses itself, and the uniqueness of our existence manifests.

If we try to make sense of this with our minds from the perspective of just this life, the only option is to go numb or die. Only when we look into our soul and see that we have lived many lifetimes, and suffered in many different ways, will we understand why we are the particular variety of fruitcake we are today—the dates come from one place, the cherries from another, the dried pineapple from another, and so on. Our minds cannot organize a hundred billion years of living.

There is one principle—let it go. That is the operational principle: Let it all go, whatever it is, because the only thing we are ever letting go is our struggle, our striving. What is real in us—what is alive, joyful, peaceful, and loving—is always with us. When we let go, we are established beyond the everyday worries of our mind in the infinite awareness that is the vibrantly peaceful source of Life Itself.

OBSTACLES

"For the most part, negative influences and obstacles are people who say one thing and do another, who spread doubt, tension....such people exist in all our lives, and we deal with them by establishing our openness on the vertical to God and then by doing the appropriate thing our openness dictates."

*I*N LIFE, THERE ARE OBSTACLES that are negative influences. These influences are negative in the sense that they are unproductive. We do not think of them as bad; we just understand that they do not bring out the best in us, which is what real love does.

For the most part, negative influences and obstacles are people who say one thing and do another, who spread doubt, tension, gossip, and generally poison the environment. We

~

have to recognize that such people exist in all our lives, and we deal with them by establishing our openness on the vertical to God and then by doing the appropriate thing our openness dictates. We have to address negative influences directly; we cannot just do the work and expect them to fall away.

It is important to deal with everyone to the degree that they are open to us and not to overextend ourselves otherwise. If we overextend ourselves, we end up creating more complication and letting more negative influences set up in our life. Not overextending ourselves can be difficult to accomplish because we want to be completely open and loving to everyone; we want to respect everybody; and openness is abundance, and abundance attracts everything. But we remember that always we are open first and foremost to the deepest part within us, to the authentic love that we are, and so we understand that in cultivating that love, it is appropriate, and to be expected, that unloving people and situations will not be a part of the flow from and within which we live.

There are ways to learn more about people so that we can appreciate them and create more of a flow. We can listen to them; we can take them to lunch, coffee, or tea. This way, we may discover someone who has finer qualities than we had imagined. Or we may discover the opposite. Maybe we will never be friends with most of the people we meet, but at least we can sort out who truly is a negative influence from a person who is just, somewhat neutrally, in our lives. But when we do encounter someone who is negative, by understanding them better, we have a chance to know how to deal with them appropriately, so as to keep discord to a minimum.

Extending ourselves to understand an obstacle is fine, but ultimately, especially in optional relationships, it is important either to separate ourselves from the negative influences or to separate them from us. There is so much real work to be done in the world on behalf of people who are truly trying to be the best they can be that there is no time to deal with people who are not deeply committed to the finest part of themselves. We are not here to hug everybody, we are here to grow. And people who are not operating with love and respect probably need to be sent, lovingly and respectfully—with a genuine sense of giving—someplace else.

KARMA

~~~

"There is no force in the universe that can constrain our potential should we choose to awaken to it. There is nothing that can limit us then, and that is when we can forget about karma."

OVER TIME, THE MEANING OF the term "karma" has changed significantly. The Buddha's idea of karma was different from the meaning the Chinese gave it, and the Japanese redefined it as well. But generally speaking, karma is that we are a woman or a man, which defines certain elements of our self-expression; it is that we are born in America or in Australia or wherever; it is our parents and their economic and social status. There are certain things about the past we cannot change—that is karma.

In our physical lives, we may not have much choice.

We struggle with a set of circumstances in which the deck is stacked against us—it is this way for everyone, rich and poor, smart and slow, beautiful and plain. Everyone has tremendous difficulties—and this is karma. Every pathway that people ordinarily pursue to a better place in this world, we must see for what it truly is, for where it will always wind up—a pathway to a plot in a cemetery. Only when we understand what we are actually doing here do we have a chance to get off the treadmill of karma and deeply experience Life. With proper support, we can completely transcend our karma. In India, which is a repressive society for women, some great women saints have come up. They had courage, were devoted—they had love and they grew. There is no force in the universe that can constrain our potential should we choose to awaken to it. There is nothing that can limit us then, and that is when we can forget about karma.

We all can be victims of our limitations, and we all have the potential to transcend them. But if we are constantly dwelling on how we are victimized, we will not have the possibility of recognizing or cultivating our profound potential. Cultivating that potential can only happen when we do not sink into the unfortunate duality of being either a victim or a violent person. The truth is, all of us are both. My teacher, Rudi, Swami Rudrananda, said there are people who eat and people who are eaten, and each of us is both. Every human being is eating and being eaten at the same time, and if we step up into a higher dimension—step back 50 miles from the process—we see this extraordinary, boiling, bubbling pot of humanity, exchanging with itself constantly, often in violent ways. The universe is unimaginably violent. The point is not to judge this process, not to dwell on our karma in all this. The point is to focus on the highest and strive for that—to live simply and straightforwardly, with love and genuine compassion in our hearts for everyone. Then we can forget about karma.

When we examine what people mean by good karma and bad karma, it usually comes down to this: the things we want and get; or the things we want and do not get and the things we do not want and do get. Yet our greater Life is not about things that happen but rather where we are within ourself in relation to those things. When we are at peace within ourself and flowing in that peace, then we

~

know that whatever the struggles, we can let go and allow them to work themselves out.

Here we are now in a beautiful place, in a beautiful time, having a beautiful moment. What else is necessary? Only that we carefully consider where we go from here. We work conscientiously to continue to cultivate the qualities that have gotten us to this moment. Then all karma dissolves. When we love our life, karma is done and so is the past.

So we continually work within ourself to raise and refine the form of ourself and the level of our practice— our interaction with others, our awareness of the dimensions of that interaction, the totality of our life. The life of Nityananda, Rudi's teacher, was different from Rudi's life, which was different from my life, and so on. We all live the life in the time and place in front of us. But when we do our work with the understanding that, at a certain point, what we are doing today will be meaningless to us down the road, we can be prepared to give it away, whatever it is—to let go of it, to walk out of it, to become a completely different person, over and over and over again.

When we continuously go back to that very subtlest

dimension of ourself, which is fuzzy because its essence is pure potential, growth, change—not structure—we are able to transcend the physical limitations of the orbit into which we were born. We are able to transcend karma.

CHILDREN

AND

RELATIONSHIPS

~~~~

"The predominant love in our life has to be within us for our

Life. Then it is possible for us to properly love, raise, and guide

our children."

A TIBETAN SAINT ONCE TALKED about our responsibility to our children by talking about our focus on the deepest part of ourself. He told the story of a male child whose parents poured all their life and love into him. These parents lived through their child, thinking that this was the best way to love him uncondi-tionally. They made decisions that adversely affected their own creative spiritual potential. But when the child grew up, he left the parents, had little contact with them, and eventually became their adversary. The parents were devastated, having neglected everything else in their life for the sake of the child. Of course, this story does not apply to many, many children, but it does emphasize the question of focus on what is truly important in life.

In raising our children, as in all our endeavors, if we are going to be the best—in this case parents—we can be, we have to have within ourself a balance, a focus on our growth, that allows us to communicate with our children their responsibility in their lives. We need to communicate to our children appropriate values that human beings live from, such as humility, compassion, clarity, and not just in words but in actions. This allows us to step back at the crucial moments and to let go—to let our children do whatever it is the creative potential, the spirit, within them wishes for them to do.

We raise our children by loving them every day and by showing them their responsibility when they mess up. The gushy part of relating to anyone is easy; it is the teaching about responsibility that is hard. But we have to hold our children to that responsibility, and we have to do this with a great deal of love and compassion. Love and compassion

~

make it possible for our children—for anyone—to deal well with responsibility.

If our children are the only love in our life, or even the predominant love in our life, this can be a problem, particularly for them. The predominant love in our life has to be within us for our Life. Then it is possible for us to properly love, raise, and guide our children.

Each person coming into this world has their own difficult work to do, and it is not possible—it is not even desirable—for us to do that work for our children. The work of each of us is to grow through all the experiences life presents us. For the sake of our children and their children, the most important thing we can do is to grow and become the best people we can be in whatever difficult circumstances life hands us.

The same is true of relationships. We have to be centered in our practice and have enough substance within ourself that we are not looking to anybody for anything in particular. We are willing to share gratefully with whomever whatever is appropriate that they bring into our life; if at some point that sharing is no longer meaningful or authentic, we need to move on with our life.

In everything, it is important not to grasp, so that the flow of Life and Its extraordinary, mysterious, gracious, and everchanging unfoldment can continue to reveal within us a stronger and deeper understanding of the essence of the whole of reality. Clarity is that essence, and with that clarity, all life is sweetness, however challenging and difficult that life might be.

Throughout the ancient Buddhist and Trika Shaiva texts, one thing is emphasized over and over again—solitude. The attachments and connections we make in our everyday life expose us to tensions, distresses, disturbances that exist in certain energy fields, and because we are interconnected with everything, that kind of disturbance disturbs us. In these disturbances, we cannot sustain clarity long enough to become completely established in it. In the tradition of Padmasambhava, who helped to bring Buddhism to Tibet in the 8th century, a three-year, three-month, three-day retreat is required on the part of every serious practitioner in order to begin to establish clarity on a permanent basis. Our approach is different, and yet we still must ask the question, "How do we sustain ourself in a serious spiritual practice in a commercial culture?" It is not easy.

When we are in the world and dealing with people, we forgo some part of our inner peace. So best to be in the world for the benefit of people, dealing with them from a place of true compassion. We are a condensation of creative power that has enormous potential to benefit the whole of humanity—our children, friends, acquaintances, people we do not even know. In Asia, some of the most elegant artistic traditions have come up in poor places where people led simple lives; and yet through endless contemplation, extraordinarily beautiful objects emerged. These objects were not intended to do anything except express the richness the artisans were digging up from within themselves and trying to bring to their everyday life—to everyone and everything in their everyday life—irrespective of meager circumstances.

It is important to strive to dig that same thing up from within ourself so that all our relationships—with our children, spouses, friends, employees, bosses, everybody with whom we share our life—can become ever deeper and more meaningful. Everything has one source, and so to look on the whole world as our children, to think about everybody, "This might be a member of my family," is the truth.

Everybody is somebody's child, and through our compassion, we relate to them as if they were the children in *our* family. After all, there is no other.

THE MYTH OF
PERSONAL CONTROL

"...How much control do we have in a life where truth is uncertainty?... Not much. And this is wonderful."

*C*HAOS AND STILLNESS ARE completely interpenetrating. This is one of the most fundamental paradoxes of existence—one of the most fundamental paradoxes of being. Chaos is also infinite uncertainty. In India, powerful and intense-looking spiritual images, such as Rudra, Bhairava, or Kali, are intended to represent chaos because the infinite is chaotic.

By contrast, in the Biblical conception of the infinite, order has been imposed upon chaos—an order which is fundamentally benevolent toward human beings as long as they do the "right" thing. It is an order that supposedly is man's prerogative by virtue of his being made in the image of God. In this system, people impress their personal sense of order on the disorder they encounter in their lives and in nature.

The Indian idea is different. It is the understanding that order and chaos are completely interdependent—they exist together. Order emerges out of chaos, dissolves into it, reemerges again and again and again. This is an understanding that has been confirmed by science: In chaos, there are patterns of order that emerge and then repeat themselves over and over. Likewise, the same chaos that exists on a universal level exists on a personal level—on a social, emotional, mental, electrical, cellular level.

Chaos is the fundamental core of everything, and change, therefore, is inevitable. Chaos exists at all levels, whether we are aware of it or not. It is one of the key features of the power that animates us—the power of spirit. We must understand that if there were anything but total uncertainty at the core of infinite creative power, it would not be infinite. Planned, ordinary, worldly life, with its many pursuits, is just something people concoct to deny the existence of that uncertainty, to struggle to reassure

~

themselves that the powerful, dark, frightening, and ex-quisite goddess at the core of the creative power, at the core of Life Itself, is not really there. So many of the drives we have to succeed and build are intended to suppress and deny uncertainty, to convince ourselves over and over again that the territory we are mapping out and the boundaries we are reinforcing ultimately secure us. This is delusion.

Change is inevitable, and the original focus of asceti-cism in spirituality was to force a shift from an obsession with security to an embrace of infinite uncertainty, which is what powers the universe, which is the power of spirit and life and transcendence. Embracing infinite uncertainty is our liberation from the treadmill, from the orbit that keeps us doing the same things to obtain a security that is an illusion. Life is forever calling upon us to adapt be-cause all living beings are compelled to do their living in a dynamic environment. When life demands an adapta-tion, the ascetic impulse, by nature unencumbered, al-lows for quick change, for a quick establishment in a new level of dynamism. The ascetic person is not attached to much, or deeply.

So the question then becomes: How much control do

we have in a life where truth is uncertainty? And the answer is: Not much. And this is wonderful.

One of the most important understandings to emerge out of the study of system dynamics is that every solution to a problem is the source of another problem. For example, if we think we are lonely, we might try to fix that by getting a relationship or drowning our sorrows in some other way. This often becomes a bigger problem than the one with which we began, because suddenly we find ourselves limited by the desires of another person with whom we are in relationship, or indulging in a drinking habit, or whatever. The short-term focus, the quick fix, leads us to a misunderstanding about life and undermines our potential for true happiness. When we try to control the outcome of everything, we are limiting the possibilities of what can happen to us to the meager visions that exist in our minds. The possibilities generated for us by the infinite—in all its uncertainty—are far richer.

In life, we have very little control over where we might end up, and this is good news. The element of change that we must start to value and even pursue in order to be in harmony with the true nature of Life Itself is a completely

~

different value from "protect, don't take risks." Continuous change means that risks are inevitable.

Most of us are told to get a college degree in order to get a good job. There is not much emphasis on pursuing an academic subject we love in order to get a job we might like—the main thrust is to be secure financially. But when we understand that life is not secure, that life is fundamentally chaotic—not the life of that person over there or this person over here but *everybody's* life, *our* life—we realize that the emphasis cannot be on anything monetary, on anything material, and this includes romantic relationships. The emphasis cannot be on security because there isn't any. The emphasis has to be on growth because growth is change at its most productive. If we are not continuously changing, learning, expanding our horizons and developing new skills, what kind of alive are we? Growth and change are synonymous, and anything that is not changing is not growing, and if it is not growing, it is dead, and that is the worst condition anything can find itself in— living and dead at the same time. We have to understand that an important part of our spiritual practice is to allow ourself, to encourage ourself, to be changed every single day by the creative potential, the power of spirit, within us.

In Hinduism, chaos is often portrayed in wrathful images that reflect, through their extreme, energetic makeup, the uncertainty persistent in real change. These are images of entities that disrespect our physical self, like the natural forces of life. These images were created by people who understood that at the highest level, we have to make peace with the uncertainty that is intrinsic in Life Itself. Having made peace, we then find value in that uncertainty because the spirit, the vitality in uncertainty, is the power by which all change takes place. It is what encourages us to grow as human beings and then to transcend our own humanity for the benefit of all that is alive.

Chaos is nothing but the power of change; it is chaotic because we cannot anticipate the outcome. If we could, how much of a change would it be? It would just be an extension of our personal agenda. And so chaos is in fact the source of our liberation—it is to be opened to, embraced; it is the opportunity for growth. Life is profoundly uncertain; change is inevitable. Out of egotism, greed, desire, ignorance, and misunderstanding, we cling to the untenable, which is what we already have. Much better to be ready to abandon what we have in a heartbeat.

I do not say this irresponsibly—because whatever is living about our lives will live on. We are always ready to abandon our current circumstance for the possibility of achieving something finer. And is there a risk in that? Absolutely. Life is about risk; chaos is the very core of our existence. Through our practice, we can stay open in the face of this core instead of allowing our defenses to come up as our minds close to the rising tide of chaos, to the rising, intensifying creative energy within and around us. Closing and reacting are attempts to impose our will on a dynamic event. History demonstrates that an attempt by one person or a group of people to impose their will on a dynamic event results, ultimately, in disaster for them and for others.

Closing and reacting are the path to doom. Opening and being aware of the flow of the power of spirit within us, which is the essence of our practice, embracing and absorbing whatever powerful energy presents itself in our life, this is the path to heaven.

WHY ARE WE HERE?

"We are here to serve each other profoundly, to give and receive from the deepest place within ourself....to participate in life in a way that releases us from all limitations. We recognize our true nature to be vast, clear, and quiet as infinite space, and we find in that...joy...."

*I*T IS IMPORTANT THAT WE ARE clear about what we are doing here. By "here," I do not mean in this room; I mean in this world, deepening a meditation practice, pursuing a spiritual life, an extraordinary life. Why are we here? We may be able to say immediately why we are not here. A spiritual life is not a good place to find romantic love, although some people do; we certainly do not exclude anything. It is not a place to advance a career, although most people do have to make a living. But the amount of energy it takes to grow—truly grow spiritually—is not going to allow us a great deal of energy to advance careers or become entangled in relationships.

What is it we are here for? We are here to have the experience of the highest possibility that exists for us. It can be summed up in one word, and that word is what all spiritual practices are about—joy. The salvation from the brutality and dimness of much of life on earth is joy. In the joyous environment created by a full and joyous heart, every kind of understanding, wisdom, exoteric and esoteric knowledge can flourish because there is a fineness in and around us that allows for this understanding to be alive in us. We are no longer stuck in our heads. In an environment of joy within us, every kind of understanding is alive; our life experience is endlessly wonderful and rich. There is a contentment in that joy that allows us to become centered in ourself, to become internally sweet and mature. It allows us to have a mind that is clear and expansive as the infinite space, a heart that is overflowing with the potentiality of dynamic stillness manifesting itself for the benefit of every living being.

~

If we are clear about what we are doing here, we still will have pressures to face. We will have to face them and not be gobbled up and complicated by them. But we confront them in order to become increasingly clear within ourself about what it is we are doing in this world. Then we can live from within ourself, above all the issues human beings drown in—perfectly clear and a beacon of that highest, clear light joy that benefits all living beings.

My time in this world grows a little bit short. I am not going to be here forever and neither are you. So it is time for us to understand: We are not here to struggle about anything but to give, from deep within ourself, authentic love, compassion, the deepest part of us, away, so that we can become completely clear and totally established in that joy that is salvation. We are here to cultivate from within ourself, in a simple and profoundly happy way, that wisdom and depth of insight that allow us to sustain this experience through time, that allow us to benefit other human beings as we live our life, finding ever more joy. We are here to participate in the transformations that take place spontaneously all around us.

We are not here to change the past; we are not here to

change the future. We are here to transcend the whole stream of tensions that make up the lives of ordinary people. We are here to endure our own karma and live above it, joyously, as we allow that dimension of our existence to exhaust itself because we are not putting energy into it by struggling.

We are here to serve each other profoundly, to give and receive from the deepest place within ourself. We are here to participate in life in a way that releases us from all limitations. We recognize our true nature to be vast, clear, and quiet as infinite space, and we find in that infinite space the joy that is the transformation of those people with whom we share our life. This is the joy of the love that we give and take as we move in this world, releasing every kind of tension and enduring every kind of difficulty. We have the capacity in this moment to become completely clear and totally joyous and to go forward from this moment to the next and the next and the next, experiencing the depth of that clarity and the richness of that joy, expanding. But we have to choose this.

We are not here to judge who is a saint and who is a sinner. We are here to see everybody as pure, creative

~

potential, moving in infinite space. We are here to transcend our karma and not to get our heads wrapped up in anyone else's. We are here to live in a clarity, a joyous love, that recognizes the unlimited essence of every human being. We are here to help every human being find that unlimited essence within themselves. And we can do this.

Yes, everyone has a hard life, but we are mistaken if we think that we are, at core, limited. We have unimaginable potential, and when we cut out any concern with our issues and get clear about what it is we are doing here—and do it—then we discover something underneath our skin truly, profoundly, special. We give to our life that profound specialness and allow it to expose us to extraordinary worlds, even as it is reaching out in so many simple ways to bless, inspire, and uplift all the people whose life it touches. My teacher, Rudi, had a harder life than any of us, and even in the face of that, he accomplished the astounding. Either we have confidence in ourself and do the work, or we continue to do whatever it is we worry about day in and day out.

Many of the most special people in human history never had a relationship or a nickel; they did not have a donkey or a pig. Maybe they had one piece of cloth. We have an intimate connection with these great people; we have a connection that has existed for centuries, millennia. These people had within themselves, within their souls, a vibrancy and expansiveness that allowed them to endure through time and space and have an impact on our present. And all of us have that same vibrancy within us. We should have no lack of confidence in ourself. We should practice and care and work and realize. And to do this, we must be clear that the joy that comes of practice, care, work, and realization is why we are here.

ATTACHMENT

We have to let go of everything we struggle to keep because we think it is good or struggle to get rid of because we think it is bad.... Realization is about becoming nothing at all.

WHAT GETS IN THE WAY OF OUR experience of joy? The simplest way to put it is—attachment. As long as we think of ourselves as individual people with individual issues and an individualized struggle, we are taking infinite spaciousness and infinite potentiality and shrinking them down to a set of limited circumstances. The fundamental reality of a human being *is* infinite space and vibrant potentiality. That is what we truly are.

Our misunderstanding about ourselves as being something other than this—a misunderstanding that leads to our attachments—comes from the idea that our bodies

~

and personalities are important. They are not. All the things people struggle to make themselves into cannot possibly succeed because we are nothing but infinite space and vibrant potentiality—infinite spirit. Our bodies will die, but what is real about us—the infinite spirit, the vibrant potentiality—will never die.

In India, the imagery and terminology of Shiva and Shakti are of Shiva as infinite space and Shakti as the vibrancy of infinite potentiality, and the two are actually one because without space, there is no vibrancy, and without vibrancy, there is no space—everything collapses. This vibrancy of potentiality is what kundalini is. The vibrancy of infinite potentiality that is Shakti, in a differentiated expression, is kundalini. And the essence of that vibrancy is joy—the joy of our own infinite spaciousness and infinite potentiality. Attachment is what causes us not to feel that joy.

Surrender is the opposite of attachment and desire. Whenever tensions arise because we think we have to be something or have something—whenever any struggle starts to happen within us—our simple response can be to give it up, let it go. Over and over again, as whatever tension between us and whomever for whatever reason comes up, before we start to engage or act out, we can give it up. This does not mean we do not act; it does not mean we do not have conflicts. But it does mean that we establish a different kind of inner environment so that our tensions do not meet those of another person and thus become a self-reinforcing set of circumstances that can only increase tension and conflict, bringing more difficulties.

Because we can flow in every circumstance in the world—because we can let it go, whatever it is—we have the possibility of living continually from a deeper place and of dissolving tensions all around us. In this way, we find real solutions to dilemmas; we release struggle and tensions; we unlock every kind of turmoil; and we allow our creative energy to rise to that level of refinement where we begin to recognize the underlying unity of the whole of life. From that experience, we find a sense of well-being, of strength; we have an inspired vision of life that we live from in an extraordinary way. And the lives of the people with whom we share our life are profoundly benefited.

Whenever we find ourselves attached and struggling, if we trust in the power of Life within us and give up the struggle, find the flow, relate to whatever the circumstance from a finer place, we will discover the joy that is the essence of our life. Only by letting go of the struggle can we reach the infinite spaciousness and joyous vibrancy of Life Itself that is within us and that we are within. We have to trust the power of spirit that gives rise to everything. There is work to be done, but much of that work is trusting in Life Itself, in the power of spirit, which allows us to come back endlessly to our balance points. Then when we are called upon to function, we will have the wisdom, discrimination, and understanding to do so.

Often, I feel my life to be ephemeral, like a cloud in motion, not set in any way. But many people are not aware of this experience in themselves. They struggle for some identity, as a child, teen, adolescent, and so on. They compress themselves into tiny balls because they identify in their heads with all kinds of problems. They are attached to an idea of themselves as having certain characteristics and therefore certain problems, and then attachment gives rise to desire, which gives rise to action, which gives rise to more karma with more suffering, which gives rise to—it is endless.

~

But truly, all that we are is not in the slightest a function of the limited circumstances in which we are existing at this moment. Thousands and thousands and thousands of years of accumulated attachment entangle us over and over again in our life in this world. And so the key is to let go—let it go, whatever it is. Our life tells us to do this over and over again, but we refuse to hear. We hold on and hold on; we struggle to hold on.

"I wish to grow" is a fine mantra, but ultimately, we have to let go of any wish. The wish to grow is the basis for letting go of all wishes, all desires. The wish to grow is productive as the basis of a commitment that rises up to become a level of devotion that has juice in it, that is sweet, rich, and real. In the form of compassion, the wish to grow rises up and encompasses the whole of humanity and all ignorance, stupidity, tension, and attachment. But this compassion is only experienced when the selflessness of devotion is realized. And that selflessness comes by letting go, because it is the ego that desires and holds on.

If we stay focused and work hard, even as we are letting go and letting go, we can work ever more deeply. We can let all the issues go so that we are able to reach within ourself for what is real and feel it and share it with other people. As long as we are attached to and struggling with our issues, issues are all we have to share. Only when we get above the issues do we find something in us that is sweet, fine, and worthy of sharing. When we share it, many people will respond positively. Some people will not, but we do not have to be confused about that. We let that go, too. Best to have a heart open so wide and a mind so quiet that the potentiality, which is our Life within, can manifest itself.

When a child comes into the world, we do not know what it is going to be. Everybody has hopes, wishes. But if we let our desires for a child get in the way of loving it, of unconditionally committing ourselves to creating the best environment in which that child can grow, what are we going to get? A lot of disappointment. A lot of tension. We have to feel about our lives the way we do about children— that we want to give them all the love and joy we can, however simple our physical circumstances. If we have appreciation for the good things that exist in our life and can nurture joy, this will allow for ever-increasingly finer things to happen, and our life will grow and with it, our joy. But in order for this to be true, we have to let go of whatever struggles and tensions arise. We have to let go of everything we struggle to keep because we think it is good or struggle to get rid of because we think it is bad.

The joy of realization only manifests in an environment of nonattachment, where we think of ourselves as nothing but infinite space and vibrant potentiality. In a state of realization, we recognize that we are not a thing but a process, a wave in infinite space. Only when we start to think about our problems do we crystallize in relationship to a set of phony circumstances. This gives rise to the very things of which we are afraid. For example, food can both nourish and poison. Money has at least two sides to it: wealth and poverty. Everything has many sides. Anything we are attached to may give rise to something we think of as good or something we feel is bad. And we do not have ultimate control over which side of the coin we are going to get. So whatever the fear, whatever the attachment—we have to let it go.

The first thing is to have some joy, and from that joy, a real life can come. Any life we get that is not based on joy is a life that is not worth living. The more we come in contact with that joy, the more fulfillment we will find within ourself; no matter what circumstances arise in our life, we find a magic that seems to make things happen, even when we know we are doing nothing at all. Realization is not about becoming great or brilliant. Realization is about becoming nothing at all.

Rudi and Nityananda talked about that nothingness; Padmasambhava talked about it, too, in slightly different terms. There is definitely a point of palpable experience in which we recognize that these things we identify as ourselves have no reality. Every condition of our human existence—our whole waking reality—is nothing more significant than a dream.

In modern physics, it has been discovered that subatomic particles have various states and that electrons have a dual state, both wavelike and particle-like. In the wavelike state, the electron does not exist in any definite place or form—or even in any definite time, because place and time are a function of one another. We are composed of trillions upon trillions of electrons—trillions upon trillions of elements that, in the wavelike state, do not exist in any definite place, form, or time. We feel we have an identity

~

in large part because we imagine ourselves in a particular way, are conditioned to certain stimuli, and respond in a specific fashion to our tensions.

Yet if we are able to rise above our conditioning and patterns of response, we can become, instantaneously, completely different people, discovering within ourself a range of potential, a range of motion, inconceivable to our brains at this moment. Everything around us is not solid, not just because it will decay and disappear at some point but because right now, like the electrons that make up this supposedly solid reality, from the perspective of the wave-like state, from the perspective of Consciousness Itself, we have but arisen briefly as a manifestation of that Consciousness. It is this simple—and this profound: We arise and we subside, every thing arises and subsides, just as dreams do. And some dreams are more compelling than others.

That level of enlightenment that is complete enlightenment is available to everyone. But we have to be committed, really committed—devoted—to that extraordinary possibility in our life. We have to have enough compassion not to dump poison on anyone—to take responsibility for and to let go of all our tensions, all our attachments, so that this enlightenment can establish itself where "me" and "mine" once was. Then we are a beacon of joy and hope for everyone.

DOUBT

"Doubt is the ground of all human suffering, of our own individual suffering. There is one way out of suffering, and that is not to wrestle with doubts or fears—or anything. It is to open our hearts and love as deeply and intensely as we can that which is present in front of us, each and every moment."

ONE DOUBT IN US CAN POISON our life. And for what? Our doubts are our way of keeping ourself separate from our life; that is all they are. They are our ego trip. This body is going to fall down; this mind is nothing more than an aggregate of perceptions and conceptions, but still we say our mind and body have great value. Still we defend them by doubting anyone or anything that threatens our perception of them. Clearly, the mind and body that give rise to doubts, concepts,

~

perceptions, judgments are not exactly real because they are not solid. We like to think of them as solid, but they are not. They change, age, die.

A spiritual life is about faith, not doubt, because, among other things, a spiritual life asks us to stop defending anything. Through our spiritual practice, we come to understand that we will not find reassurance in form; we will not find nourishment there. Nourishment is in the essence, the source, and we find reassurance in the power of our contact with that source—a contact that will transform us and our life profoundly. Doubt is fear and struggle. When the mind is released from fear and struggle, what is revealed is infinite potentiality.

In Biblical cosmology, creation is an effect of a conscious action; the world is intentionally built in a certain way by God, who had this idea and acted on it. The Indian notion is quite different. In the Indian view, the world is an extension of a manifestation of the presence of God, a reflection of the vitality intrinsic to that presence. Rather than being a structure established in the beginning that was carried on, reasserting itself through aeons according to the will of some "other," life, to the Indians, is constantly changing, unfolding, manifesting itself in layers, like the waves manifest themselves from the ocean.

And so rather than being an effect, the mind is an extension of infinite power. As Rudi used to say, the mind, in its concrete form, is "the slayer of the soul"; in its essence, it is an extension of the power of the soul, which is a manifestation of the vitality of the infinite. When the mind is released from its struggle with the paradoxes of life—with the contradictions we experience in the world and within ourselves—the mind is free to examine its own source. What is revealed is infinite potentiality. All the doubts, fears, and tensions most people cultivate reflect a poverty of spirit, not the richness of the potential within us, which is the power of spirit.

In India, that power of spirit is figured forth in various deities, but these are not separate entities. We may think that in India, there are thousand of gods and that in the Judeo-Christian tradition in which most Americans are raised, there is only one God; but it is not like that. In India, there are a thousand gods representing a thousand forms of the one God—or a million forms or a billion forms. Perhaps even the form that is inside each of us.

When we realize that the power of spirit is within us, to what do our everyday issues amount? How much do those issues have to do with us becoming the biggest person we can be? Issues usually are about defending a small territory, not about being bigger. If we do not free our minds from the issues, from the disappointments—which in every case arise because we have succumbed to some fear and doubt—how will we ever be the best person we can be? How will we discover even a small amount of the extraordinary potential hidden within us? Most of us have experienced feedback that is not positive. But how many of us realize that the places where we do get positive feedback, which we generally gravitate towards, are often circumstances that limit us? They do not ask much of us, and so we do not rise to the highest occasion.

Continuous growth does not come by defending our issues. Continuous growth comes by rising endlessly to a vision of the deepest potential in us and working to manifest that potential in the face of whatever tensions and resistance, obstacles and limitations we might face. It is only by having some deep commitment to the best person that resides within us—and working continuously to express

~

that person—that life has any richness to it, any sweetness, any lightness, or life in it at all.

Life is a paradox. There is everything in everything, and if we cannot rise to the level within ourselves where we are very big people, then it will be impossible to find peace in the context of this paradox. We will never make true sense out of it because perhaps it was not created in a sensible manner. Perhaps like almost everything created with even a semblance of functioning, it was created a fifth by design and eighty percent by accident.

When I am in Nepal, I do certain ritual practices in the cremation grounds. These are ancient practices done in the places that are the boundary between this world and the next, between this life and the next. The people of ancient times who deeply practiced yoga and pursued the ultimate reality pursued their meditation in places like the cremation grounds. In their meditation practice, these practitioners sacrificed their body and energy for the benefit of others—to ease the suffering of human beings and other living creatures and to uplift them. In making this sacrifice, the practitioners of ages past as well as those of today recognize that after they have given away everything possible, including body and mind, they are still here. After everything they think they have is gone, what they really have is still present, and in fact, it is so present that it is unobstructed or unencumbered in any way. What is gone is doubt—their own suffering, clinging, attachment. All worries are dissolved.

There is an underlying unity between suffering and great joy. All thoughts—whether positive or negative, moral or immoral, ethical or unethical, selfish or profoundly generous—ultimately have an underlying unity to them, and they are self-liberating. When we see through our doubts and fears to this underlying unity, we understand why great beings are often portrayed in spiritual literature as frustrated by the endless capacity of human beings to stay small—to cling to their issues—and to keep suffering even though there is the infinite possibility within their suffering to become released.

We have an amazing possibility. Centered, free of doubt, totally focused—not out of selfish need but out of devotion—we are able to appreciate the unlimited expanse of pure creative power present within and around us at all times. That experience makes us realize how our worries

~

are actually nonsense. Everybody's issues are born in their own head—in that concrete mind that is the slayer of the soul—and these issues have no reality beyond that.

The essence of spiritual growth is to sacrifice ourself to our highest Self. When I was a boy in Catholic school, I was taught to love God. And I kept loving God and *really* feeling that love, and I realized that the love within me was growing, and it was not love for a transcendent, supreme being—I was loving that love, which grew and grew and grew. But we cannot cultivate that love and cultivate doubt at the same time.

Doubt is the ground of all human suffering, of our own individual suffering. There is one way out of suffering, and that is not to wrestle with doubts or fears—or anything. It is to open our hearts and love as deeply and intensely as we can that which is present in front of us, each and every moment. Not clinging to it and grabbing for it. Not repelled by, scared of, doubtful of, and judging it. Just loving it, being open to it.

We are here to free ourselves from our misunderstandings—not by doubting our life or being afraid of it or of anybody else in our life. We free ourselves from all misunderstandings by loving our life, by respecting the people in it, all the people in all their diverse forms and ways, growing in our understanding of them and of everything, as the trauma, doubt, fear, and tension with which we walked into this world fall out of us.

Then we are not running away from anything, wanting anything, afraid of anything, in doubt about anything. Our minds are perfectly clear. Everything is simply pure, unlimited, completely clear loving presence—the presence of God, the power of spirit.

The tradition of sannyasa in India is not a life-denying process because at the end of all the vows of renunciation, sannyasis renounce renunciation. Still, the vows speak to the idea of removing oneself from experience, of a withdrawal. But the Indian Kaula tradition, in which kundalini yoga is the core practice, is a complete celebration of Life because from this nondualistic perspective, there can be no withdrawal. There can be no renouncing anything because everything is implicit within one pure essence of authentic Life that is the core of our soul.

Renunciation or sannyasa says, "Leave it all"; Kaulism says, "Love it all." Sannyasa says, "Just walk away from it;

~

it's all an illusion." Kaulism says, "Engage in everything appropriate to an authentic Life. In the immanent, there is the transcendent, and in the transcendent, the immanent. The two are inseparable." There is no other.

And so we understand that there is no life condition that is intrinsically limiting of our spiritual pursuit. Whatever life process unfolds from within us as a function of our contact with that authentic place within is perfect. There is only one poison, and that is doubt. Doubt is the poison that spoils Life.

So we put down our egos, worries, fears, doubts—we put all that aside and allow the extraordinary potential within to express itself. Spiritual growth is not about tomorrow or the next day, or liberation in the future. The time is now. The challenge for each of us is to make our life a life worth living, a life filled with love and joy and wonder—now. And it is possible. But instead of defending issues, we have to turn our attention to the challenge of being a truly big person and rise to that challenge. There is nothing to figure out except that we are here to love, not to doubt.

TRUST THE PROCESS

"Our life is not about being any place in particular or in some different circumstance than what the process has given us; it is about being within ourself."

*A*UTHENTIC PRACTITIONERS of yoga are people who have given over all their desires to the highest creative potential that exists within them. That potential exists everywhere, but it manifests in our life from within ourself. Once we are established in our commitment to grow spiritually, the next step is to trust the process.

Yoga practice is about surrender, not about the renunciation or the desiring of anything. Yoga practice is about the continuous releasing of our hopes and fears into the flow of the creative power within us. It is about learning to trust that power. When we are in touch with that power, it is difficult to act in a way that is not ultimately in the best interest of the whole.

Surrender means surrendering struggles, tensions. It is not about surrendering any particular thing. We should always be peacefully floating above the waves. Struggle gives rise to desire, and ultimately the lack of trust in Life Itself gives rise to struggle. If we can start to feel the creative power within us in the most simple, physiological way, which is the fluctuation of the cerebrospinal fluid as well as the breath, we have a reference point to begin to relate to that highest creative power within. We begin to trust that it will bring its own extraordinary understanding and benefit to our entire life. If from that simple point, we can let go and let that benefit happen, it does. It does not happen in a straight line. Sometimes that benefit seems fast and flashy, sometimes it manifests slowly, as a tide of the creative power breathing its own breath of God, resolving strain and stress, tension and trauma, bringing peace. First it brings peace, then it brings joy, then it brings complete understanding.

All yoga is about being aware of, living from, and trusting divine power. Divine power is infinitely wise. There is a wisdom to each person's destiny and a process by which divine power manifests itself fully from within each person. This process is to be respected. Each of us needs to respect the logic of divine power manifesting itself in the form of the life that we have, and that everyone has, and to stop looking elsewhere. This means we stop having any ideas that there is some place better for us to be than where we are.

Blocks in us develop when we want something to happen and work hard to make it happen, and it does not happen, so we work harder at it. We pour loads of energy into it, and all we get is a powered-up tension. Tension goes to tension. So we have a block, instead of what we wanted, because maybe what we wanted was not a fit for us in the first place. It did not, after all, emerge from the basic harmony in us but from a figment of our imagination that we turned into a life issue.

What is important in our life is our contact with the power of spirit within us and our openness to that power's spontaneous manifestation of its own extraordinary wisdom in the form of our life in this moment, in the next moment, in the next, and in the next. To be aware of and to trust that highest creative power—to celebrate all transitions as an expression of it and to trust it to unfold from within us its highest state of total well-being—this is not easy, but it is essential to yoga practice.

So yoga in one of its simplest and profoundest forms is dependence on that creative power within us. It is transcending our desires, allowing Life to demonstrate Its own infinite potentiality from within as we practice a fundamental, basic understanding when we move through this world. If we care and continue to do our work, this extraordinary power of Life will bring into the field of our life the support appropriate to our growth, which may not be instantly recognizable. It will take some faith just to trust the process. It is not about another person doing something for us but what we can do with the raw material presented to us in our life; it is up to us always to come back to the basic point of what kind of person it is we want to be and what kind of work we are willing to do to unfold the creative, visionary potential that lies deep within us.

~

Every kind of understanding that will ever be useful to us is already, in a subtle way, embedded within us, and our challenge is to keep our attention deeply within ourself long enough that we can allow this understanding to emerge. Being involved in the tensions, struggles, issues, desires, hopes, fears, concepts, goals of a life agenda we insist on creating only means that what we are really doing is denying ourself Life. We can feel, and by feeling, strengthen, the spirit within us. As that spirit becomes stronger, it is important to trust it in our everyday life so that we can learn to live within ourself as a growing human being—an expanding, spiritual presence—rather than struggling in reaction to the difficulties we encounter. Every day, all I am doing is serving God in the way I am called on to do and having great trust in the creative power to bring about its own perfection in all who will allow it.

The deities of nondualistic, Hindu spiritual practices are not about anything "out there." They are about qualities and capabilities intrinsic to the creative power within us. The feeling of that power leads us to begin to cultivate a trust in, a reliance on, that power within ourself, and this trust expands our consideration, thoughtfulness, and compassion.

Life presented us here, and we do not get to say what for or for how long. The fundamental power in us has a rhythm of its own, and when we attune ourselves to it, we trust it. Then we do not have to be any place that is different from where we are; we just have to get to work and let that power take us wherever it wishes. When we live in a state of surrender, we have no resistance to the movement of that power as it carries us. It will take us to places we may not want to leave and then jerk us from there to places we wish we had missed. And the only thing to do is to live from and sustain a profound state of surrender as this highest creative power unfolds its capacity within the total field of our life. This power will take us where it wishes anyway. And we all probably have experienced the extraordinary tension of resisting it. There is no denying ultimate reality.

We have to learn to trust the process. Trusting the process is the only way that liberation has a chance of coming to us in the brief span of one lifetime. That is much better than the ten thousand aeons that many have wandered aimlessly in this world, suffering and contributing to the suffering of other people. If it just takes us one lifetime now, that is profound good fortune.

~

If we do not trust the process, then our egos bleed into our endeavor and undermine us completely. Our lack of trust means we have no confidence, and when the important moments of realization come, we will doubt ourself and lose the power of those moments. In meditation, in yoga practice, some energy reorganization happens, and it happens inside us. Something comes to us; some vision happens, and we get clear about who we are and what all this is, and how it is connected. But if we do not trust the process, our spiritual life is spoiled.

Trusting the process requires patience and perseverance. This is not a ninety-day deal. What kind of depth as a human being would we manifest and what kind of character would we develop if all we believed in was the quick fix? What strength would we have with which to hold in our nervous system a vision of and contact with ultimate reality? It takes strength.

Trust the process. It may be difficult to do, and the people we meet still will not fit into our rational model of what we want them to be; things still will not satisfy us. But in trusting the process, we will come to see that the process itself is wonderful. So many of our tensions dissolve; we can practice in peace, and this is important.

Being at peace within ourself is the essential ground of our spiritual life, of our growth. Without peacefulness within, we are just spinning our wheels. When we trust the process, we can reflect on the whole of humanity with compassion. In that peaceful compassion, a true state of surrender—our life in God—happens. Then we are no longer prisoners of the mantra that most people keep repeating with ever-increasing self-absorption, "What's going to happen to me? What's going to happen to me? All I care about is, what's going to happen to me?" Being peaceful, we experience the joy our contact with the place of wholeness, clarity, and well-being within ourself brings. Because we are trusting of the process, we are peaceful, and our mind is quiet and our awareness *is* that contact.

If we are caught up in desires, we know automatically that we do not trust the process, because when we really trust our Life, we take what It gives us. It will give us some things we want and many we do not, and what it does not give us has nothing to do with the deepest part of us unfolding itself. When we trust the process and are at peace, the real benefits of our practice start to happen.

~

While we may trust the process, we will not necessarily trust all the people we meet, and that is appropriate. Trusting the process has nothing to do with the agendas of people. But while we might have doubts about such things in our lives, we cannot have doubts about the Life process that is our source and the source of everyone and everything. We accept that God has placed everything in our life that is there and every circumstance for us to open to and to live with in as much peace as we possibly can. This we do in order that all tensions, complexity, and trauma of aeons of accumulated life experience can come together and be resolved in a way that allows us to transcend this endless cycle of suffering. Then our growth and transcendence benefit everybody whose life our life touches. If we distrust the process and are not at peace, we are only thinking about ourselves, and then we will, most likely, not benefit anyone.

We do not want to suppress anything. Trusting the process is not about denying anything. It is about becoming quiet and clear. It is about allowing the power of Life within us, which has brought us to this moment, to fulfill itself in this lifetime and to bring us, within ourself, to the greatest happiness possible. Not trusting the process and not practicing in peace cause us to imagine that there is something to be done, when there is nothing to do. It causes us to go endlessly into the darkness and find for our effort only disappointment.

Our life is not about being any place in particular or in some different circumstance than what the process has given us; it is about being within ourself. It is not about getting information from a teacher; it is about sustaining a contact, with the help of the teacher, which allows for the field of tension around us to dissolve and for that highest creative power within to unfold. Then we see that a life that trusts the process can only bring out the best in us.

THE RELIGION
OF THE LAW,
THE SPIRITUALITY
OF LOVE

~

"One major difference between religion and spirituality is the notion of an unchanging truth versus the truth is *change.... Spirituality says the truth is reciprocal with change.... The power of spirit recreates us, and in living from and within it, it shows us and teaches us from within ourself."*

SPIRITUALITY IS DIFFERENT from the practice of religion. Religion tries to impose an artificial, mental map—a belief system—on its followers. The system is there to bring order into a person's life, which is an attempt to avoid pain. But spirituality is not as interested in order as it is in growth and in a state of completeness that has an internal harmony, encompassing *all* forms of experience. Spirituality is about bringing a fresh mind every day to our life and from within ourself attempting to feel what is authentic and vital and to express it in accord with our environment. This takes a lot of practice.

Spirituality is not about judging anyone; it seeks to learn. If we have a belief system that says, "This is right and that is wrong," then automatically it means that everyone who does not think the way we do has some inherent defect in them. Then, we might not be allowed to learn about or from them, or even to be exposed to them, for fear that in some way, their inherent defect will be inserted into us.

Such a system over time produces small, tight human beings. In that contracted state, opportunities for the accumulation of pathology and for manifesting violence—because of the lack of internal flow—are increased, and the suffering that happens as a result is profound. Nowhere in such a model is there the possibility of every form of experience being included in a harmonious, stable, all-encompassing event. Rather than a set of rules as our touchstone, which unfortunately is what so many formal religions provide, we need first and foremost an open heart and mind. Rules and regulations over time are going to cause us to contract in order to live within narrow boundaries, and this encourages inharmonious suppression rather than creative expression.

A spiritual person wants to create an environment around and within themselves where they can grow, where they can begin to recognize everything that they are as it all comes together and functions as a living whole. A spiritual person takes in everything—all difficulty, everything—and grows from it. It is important to be compassionate and not judgmental because any experience can be positive or negative; experience itself is neutral. In the process of taking in the difficult experiences, we try to recognize that a part of any difficulty has something to do with a piece of ourself that is unfolding, so we constantly keep our hearts and minds open. When we are in such a state of compassion, what is trying to change within us and to shift in the environment can do so, without suppression.

As spiritual people, we see the need to be compassionate

〜

to ourselves and others, and in doing this, we are not justifying our own eccentricities. Rather, compassion keeps us open and learning about Life. We want to learn about ourself, about people. We see that Life is not narrow and that an ordinary mind cannot fathom It. So we want to understand the profoundly complex and sophisticated event we see around us. We practice for years and years from an authentic place—not a tense and judgmental place—to begin to come to some appreciation of the vastness of Life and of Its extraordinary elegance.

I have said and will say many times: Life is a paradox; this paradox is what we are striving to know, understand, and embrace as spiritual people. Life is both real and unreal at the same moment; it is substantial and nonexistent at once. Think of it like this: How real is something that is constantly and forever changing? Rapidly and furiously changing.

We are changing much more dynamically than we can readily appreciate, but in the practice of religion, the awareness of this uncontrollable change that is the fundamental core of our existence is suppressed because that suppression makes us think everything is manageable. The problem with this perspective is that we are denying ourselves access to vast dimensions of creative potential within us.

An imaginary creative life is a life of the mind. The extraordinary creative life is the recreative life of the soul, and that recreative life is remaking us entirely, recreating us and our life completely on a regular basis. One major difference between religion and spirituality is the notion of an unchanging truth versus the truth *is* change. Many religions stand on tradition and speak to what they imagine to be the unchanging truth of that tradition. Spirituality says the truth is reciprocal with change, and the reality is that we are completely recreated many times in our lives, and countless times over aeons. The power of spirit recreates us, and in living from and within it, it shows us and teaches us from within ourself.

When we deny ourselves access to vast parts of the information that exists within us about ourself and Life, how thoughtful are we capable of being in dealing with people we love? How thoughtful are we going to be in acting out the various releases of tension and poison within us? If we are denying ourselves access to the whole, how will we express our growth carefully and appropriately?

Life is a paradox; it is one thing one moment, another the next. And we are paradoxes. The strangeness that we see about all life is real: Life is strange. This paradox only has a resolution in a state of complete openness, where all parts of the dynamic event that is Life Itself are free to function fully and in the harmony that It is. It is a harmony that is vast, not a small harmony, meaning there are parts of It that are disharmonious even as there is a much broader environment in which much of the dissonance works together. But if we only allow ourselves to appreciate and tune into just so much and no more, what are we going to be? We are going to end up being tighter and tighter, smaller and smaller, searching for a certainty that exists nowhere. A state of liberation is the resolution of the paradox of Life in its complete, in its most vast, in its whole sense—in an awareness that does not fit into any container.

The religion of the law says that if we do this and that— and do it this way and that way—God will promote us at the end of our days. For many people, this is important. If people have some sense of certainty, if they feel that doing everything right will get them a sure result, then even when their actions are not necessarily for the highest benefit of everyone concerned, they do not think it matters. But the spirituality of love says something different. It says that this soul, which is the essence of our existence, comes into this world for a purpose, and that purpose is to grow so that this soul, which is our essence, can express itself completely and unto its own fulfillment and, therefore, become free of the entanglements, tensions, and suffering of this world. The religion of the law does not allow for our soul to grow. It puts everybody's soul into a box and says, "This is the way it has to be." Not one of us fits into the box. Not one of us is the way we are constantly told we are supposed to be.

We have to be able to make mistakes, to see where we do not fit into the box, to accept ourselves and in taking responsibility for our mistakes, become a bigger person. For me, the essential quality we have as a person who wants to grow—who cares about their life, soul, and the quality of life around them—is the ability to take responsibility for our mistakes. If we cannot say, "These mistakes are mine," if we cannot learn from our mistakes and change ourselves because of them, we will blame everybody else for the pain we experience, whereas it is nobody's fault. It is what life is. The pain we experience is our human condition, which we are transcending through our ability to reach within to find something deeper and finer, loving and caring.

Spiritual people who transcended everything, including the box of religion, were, and are, Mahasiddhas. They are neither monks nor family people; they are considered to be specialists, people who are unusual in that they have some unique achievement within themselves that they have no particular intention of passing on; they represent no tradition. There are no practices in which they are obliged to engage. They have no particular discipline to follow, no particular dress, no vows to keep—nothing. The Mahasiddhas are people who have a commitment to the realization of the Ultimate Reality, which transcends any obligation to conform to, or in any way to attempt to benefit, the whole of society.

One of the functions of religion is to stabilize society into social groups. Religion attempts to alleviate some of the anxiety people feel when they encounter uncertainty, which is every single moment of every single day.

~

Mahasiddhas, on the other hand, have a profound commitment to grow, which causes them to embrace change and to accept uncertainty. This is not the kind of public teaching that generally wins great popularity and therefore transforms society.

Historically, Mahasiddhas did not identify themselves with any one religious way. Nityananda, an Indian saint of this century who was the teacher of my teacher, Rudi, used various religious terms: He spoke in the language of his place in India, and he also used terminology that might be considered Trika Shaiva. Padmasambhava, the Mahasiddha who helped to bring Buddhism to Tibet in the 8th century, was a synthesizer, taking from several traditions, including Shaivism. But the Mahasiddhas had one thing in common: Their position in general was that in each moment, every moment is. In each moment, every moment.

One must respect all religions and appreciate any religious practice anybody wants to undertake. We are particularly appreciative of the people upon whom these religious traditions are founded. The difficulty comes in the tendency of organizations to perpetuate their own interests over the interests of the people from whom these organizations evolved as well as over the interests of human beings these organizations are intended to serve.

The Kashmirian theologian, aesthetician, spiritual teacher, and Tantric practitioner, Abhinavagupta (circa 1000 C.E.), said that religious traditions need to reinvent themselves from time to time, and he was definitely the preeminent commentator of his day, if not of his entire tradition. But today we think it is important in religious traditions to carry on in the present and sustain in the future what was done in the past. Yet, as Abhinavagupta firmly believed, the vitality of a tradition may depend upon the thoughtful reinvention of itself over and over again. Padmasambhava reinvented Buddhism in Nepal in the 8th century and continued the reinvention in Tibet. He did this in a fashion appropriate to the culture.

From the Mahasiddhas, who freely engaged, without regard for tradition and mandate, in spiritual practices in order to discover and express the power of spirit within them, we understand that unchanging tradition may not be productive, at least from a spiritual point of view. The reason is simple: Whether we know it or not, we come to a spiritual practice to some degree to be liberated from our personal history. We want to transcend our tradition of underachieving in our lives, of constantly reaching for something we think is going to be life-enhancing only to find it a disappointment. We are trying to be liberated from that tradition. So, too, religious traditions have to be liberated from their pasts. Otherwise, they become like government institutions, or any institution—self-serving, small, inwardly oriented in a fashion that does not promote growth but sustains structure. Governments do this— corporations, even relationships.

In most spiritual traditions, there is an emphasis on good works, on charity, on outward forms, such as singing, chanting, bowing, praying, the offering of flowers. What is the point of this? Is it lifeless tradition in all cases? The answer is, no. These outward forms promote devotion, and deeply one-pointed devotion leads to clarity. The ultimate goal of a spiritual practice, and of all the outward practices of it, is to live in perfect clarity. One of the things to be appreciated most about Buddhism is that over the centuries, the Buddhists have worked hard to develop a well-organized and systematic training program for people of clarity.

Laws exist to regulate commerce between people on all levels. Laws do not exist between God and man, contrary to the doctrine of certain traditions. If God is infinite—truly, truly infinite—how can there be any laws in that? If God is infinitely loving, what rules will there be?

Laws are about commerce, and likewise, the rules in the religion of the law are about making a deal with God: "If I do this and this, then You'll be nice to me here and in the hereafter." A spiritual practice is not about making deals with God, and it is not about making deals with each other. It is about finding that fundamental ground upon which all experience manifests and finding our own essence as harmoniously interconnected with the essence of the whole of Life. A spiritual practice is about loving and being loved, period. And that transcends every kind of deal.

THE UNION OF POWER
AND COMPASSION

"...if we contact from within us the whole of infinity, then we understand. We know there is nothing out there, nothing— there is no power to acquire because the power of spirit is already within us. And that power is about compassion."

WHEN WE TALK ABOUT "THE power of spirit," the word "power" may make some people edgy. People are comfortable with the idea of compassion implied by the word "spirit," but not so comfortable with the idea of a relationship between power and spirit. So it is important that we discuss the true nature of power itself. Power and compassion are both about flow. In the case of some religions, as with many governments and politicians,

~

power has been about limitation, about concentrating energy in the hands of a few people. But what good is power if it does not flow? Think about it carefully. Is power truly powerful if it is not flowing?

If we have power, why would we want to hold onto it, hold it in? That is just constipation, in this case, spiritual constipation. The ultimate power, after all, is not acquired; it is already within us. It is creative power, which is the unfoldment of the power of spirit, or the power of the Self, or the dynamic stillness, the motion that exists in space—and it articulates its own program.

When we talk about power, we are seeking to free our thinking from any kind of egoistic attachment to the idea of power. True power is and true power does; an individual human being can do nothing but limit the function of it. So we sacrifice, give up our ego and attachments, in order that the power of spirit can articulate its full potentiality within the field of our view. It articulates its power in our life and expresses its own design. Because of the simplicity, devotion, and clarity we cultivate within ourself, we see this and participate in the profound richness of that potentiality unfolding itself from within us.

~

It is power, we cannot deny that, because everything is becoming transformed within and around us. Wonderful things happen. But if we confuse ourselves with that power, or strive in some way to touch that power with our egos, then it will be unpleasant. So we arrive at the state of clarity within us and look into the hearts and souls of other human beings from that clarity and then use the power that we have within to take on the suffering of other human beings, to take it in. In taking the suffering of other human beings onto us, helping them to find the deeper state of clarity within themselves, we make possible for many, even if it is just for a little while, a different sense of value for themselves and a different sense of the possibilities in their life. And so the ultimate power is about compassion. We are here to serve the highest potentiality for total well-being that exists within every person. The power of spirit is about compassion.

The point is, power for what? I have seen people in India and other countries who can manifest apples out of socks. They can make mountains of incense ash from nothing or materialize watches and diamond rings. There are many people who have such power. But such a magic show is about money.

The Tantric perspective is: Have every experience and recognize in all experience that all experience leads to suffering save one; that one experience is the complete contact with the power of Life Itself, the perfect clarity, that is within us. If we think of it as being only within the "me," we make an important mistake, but if we contact from within us the whole of infinity, then we understand. We know there is nothing out there, nothing—there is no power to acquire because the power of spirit is already within us. And that power is about compassion.

I have immense respect for every religion; and what we are concerned to do in our spiritual practice, regardless of religion, is to find within ourself that state that is free from misunderstanding and to speak from that state to the special, profound, beautiful, divine, complete, whole quality—whole power—that exists in all of us. In speaking to that, we can give nourishment so that this power can come alive in every arena our life touches.

Life is made better by attending to that part of life that is truly profound, truly powerful. Filling ourself with the experience of clarity and love that makes life delicious brings happiness and peace into the lives of all those people

~

with whom we share our life. It is hard to hold onto the powers of a business empire, or onto a bucket of money, or onto whatever, when our body disintegrates; such things are not truly powerful. The only true power in this world or out of it is the power of spirit, and it is also the power that speaks to and from compassion for all.

SALVATION

❧

"Salvation is that we are able to go beyond ourselves, to go

beyond our tensions and judgments to see in people that which

is kindred and living in the connection of that kindredness."

*T*HERE IS A POPULAR EXPRESSION
in spiritual practice about the path to enlightenment, to
salvation. The phrase is "the secret teaching," and implicit
in the idea is a one-step, effortless shortcut to eternal para-
dise. But the secret teaching is in fact the opposite. The
essence of it is what my teacher, Rudi, used to call "depth
over time," or sacrifice, and that is because sacrifice is the
effective act that connects a human being to their source.

Sacrifice is not a ritual act. It can happen in a ritual
context, but for the most part, the ritual is an educational
paradigm—a metaphor. The actual ritual act is a metaphor for the way in which we should live our everyday

~

life. Ritual can be an effective act in itself, but it is intended to point us towards the awareness of a life process that gives vitality to the ritual act and extends it throughout the entire field of our awareness. In this way, we are constantly expanding our contact with our own source.

Religions talk about salvation, and when they do, they are speaking to the capacity to have meaningful interchange, to be nourished through and to nourish our life experience, which is first our deep contact with ourself and then our contact with everyone. Salvation is that we are able to go beyond ourselves, to go beyond our tensions and judgments to see in people that which is kindred and living in the connection of that kindredness.

In emphasizing the unity of the Holy Trinity, Christianity is putting forth a model for that kindredness. The Father represents universal consciousness, the source of nourishment in the universe. The Son is a manifestation of the unlimited whole. The connection between the Father and the Son is Spirit, which is the means of communication for the two—the universal, the manifestation of the universal in the limited, and the energetic connection in the middle. This could be a guru-disciple-grace

~

model, or, for the nondualistic Shaiva practitioner, the model of subject, object, and means of cognition. What these models express is the total unity of individual consciousness coming from absolute consciousness and the energetic connection between the two, which makes it one reality.

The recognition of and the living from the realization of this unity bring about a transformation that is salvation. In Catholic terms, this means saved from sin. But sin only has meaning when someone is operating in bad faith, when the individual is so absorbed in themselves that they have no relationship to the larger universe in which they operate. Having no relationship to the larger universe, they are stumbling around breaking everything, making a mess of whatever they do, hurting people's feelings, only worried about themselves, thinking that they are the sole event. This is sin.

Some people think that salvation comes when they have made a lot of money or have realized some desire. These people think that God is showing the rightness of their actions by rewarding them with material things. One need only look at a saint such as Nityananda, and the simple way in which he lived, to realize the delusion in this line of thinking.

To recognize kindredness is the key to salvation. Instead of blaming, criticizing, and judging everyone—instead of judging the success of our life process and the life process of anyone else by how many desires have been fulfilled—we cultivate discipline and communication skills, and we take responsibility for our life. Above all, we have great patience, with ourselves and everyone. These are the means to salvation.

In order to connect to kindredness, we have first a connection to ourself. It is impossible to connect to anyone else if we do not have that. This takes work. Rudi emphasized work, and his students understood that we work to contribute something of value that creates the possibility for us to experience the kindredness of spirit.

It is important, though, to understand that work does not mean struggle. In infinite space, all things are self-liberating; salvation is our natural state. Every form arises and subsides, returns to the essence, the source, over and over and over again. So from the perspective of infinite space, we do not really "work" at anything, in the sense

~

of struggling or pushing to achieve something. We already are that something—deeply are that something—and we only need to reach through this form that has manifested to find the essence of what we truly are and to live from that.

Surrender and sacrifice are interrelated, and so when we cultivate kindredness, we sacrifice material goals, objectives, long-term planning regarding our corporate existence. Instead, we rely on the kindredness that is spirit—surrendering to that connection, relying on that connection to reveal itself as it goes along, as we are nourishing it, in the same way a child reveals itself over time. Just as with a child, while we may have a plan, it has to be a loose one, or we will suffocate what we are trying to nurture. No plan at all, of course, is equally unproductive.

As spirit unfolds itself, it reveals its own life, which we are attending to, rather than thinking endlessly of ourselves. This brings about the highest experience, according to all religious scriptures. We feel our life saved from the treadmill that is dominated by money and recognition. In sacrifice, the possibility of real expansion—which has nothing to do with expanding our territory, money, or recognition—takes place. The result of focusing on getting something is constipation, not expansion. Such a person becomes constipated by materialism of every kind.

Materialism is not entirely an unproductive thing. A beautiful environment, such as the one we have at the Nityananda Institute, can be a source of true inspiration. But this environment has come about because many people contributed something of value from within themselves, and this is an event where that value will live on and be increased, refined; it will evolve. This evolution will not come about if we are thinking about taking anything; it will come from focusing on giving. It will come from the sacrifice we make as we break down our tensions, doubts, and cynicism, and open to, surrender to, and live with any pain, in a way that allows us to have authentic maturity. From this maturity, we can appreciate the value of sacrifice, the significance of giving, as an act more satisfying than getting anything.

Sacrifice continuously reestablishes our connection with ourself. Without sacrifice, tensions grow and become barriers between people. Without sacrifice, barriers between people crystallize into complete breakdowns in

~

communication, into misunderstanding and even hatred, violence.

Sacrifice takes us out of a self-absorbed state in order to appreciate that the world does not exist just for the opportunity of *our* eating and reproducing, *our* desiring and acquiring. It is a larger, dynamic environment that is forever transforming and reforming ourself so that we constantly remake our connection to something that is constantly remaking us. In order to stay in a truly meaningful place within ourself, in order to feel the salvation that is already present within us—the liberation that is already ours— we are sacrificing.

Life is a process by which we are continuously unfolding the vibrant potentiality within us and through which we are experiencing, in spite of the confusion of life, some extraordinary joy. This is salvation. But it does not come from molding ourselves into an image of which others approve; it comes from our contact with who we deeply and truly are. Saving our life is not about behaving according to a standard code; it is not about being saved from sin. Life is not controllable, and for so many people, it is brutal; and so we have to be completely open-minded and openhearted, even as we hold to the fundamental principles of our commitment and devotion to, as well as our compassion for, all living beings. Saving our life is about having a life worth living because we are living it from the power of spirit within us. That is a saved life. That is salvation.

RITUAL AND PURITY:
THE HAVAN

"The offering we make in the havan is our individual awareness into the infinite awareness.... We bring sweetness and love in our heart, and we are offering this sweetness and love into the Life process that we are so that this process can grow on its own, expand, become powerful, and be the energy field in which we live."

A HAVAN, WHICH IS A HINDU ritual fire ceremony, is intended to create a change of state. The point of focus is the fire, which tells us that we are not a thing but a process. The havan is about recognizing that we have extraordinary, divine gifts within us. The offering of sweet things into the fire—flowers, nuts, fruit—

is a metaphor for calling forth from within us some sweetness and offering it with love. This flow of sweetness and love leads to the experience of the profoundly sacred.

As part of the ceremony, there are sounds, such as the chanting cadence of mantras interspersed with instruction about prayers, as well as the spitting and crackling of the constantly fed fire. The things that are offered create specific smells as they burn, and this particular pungency is one reason why certain items are considered the most appropriate offerings. The environment becomes permeated with the smell of the smoky fruit, nuts, and flowers and with the vibration of the prayers, and we find ourself immersed in a dynamic energy. Superficially, we may feel a little buzzy, and then, ever more deeply inside, we start to feel wonderfully stirred up. This fire ritual is an external event that becomes internalized.

The deities who are part of the fire ceremony are the elephant god, Ganesha, who removes all obstacles in a person's path to spiritual growth, and goddesses such as Chandi, Lakshmi, and Saraswati. The Shiva Lingam and Nataraja are also part of the ritual. The significance of these elements is to recognize the infinite qualities, the universal

~

qualities, that exist within every human being. The deities are not entities that are seen as "other," as differentiated from us. For example, Ganesha and the guru are considered to be one and the same; the guru removes obstacles in our understanding on the way to the pure experience of ourself and the unfoldment of our highest potentiality.

The havan sets up an energy field that respects the universal, creative qualities of graciousness, generosity, courage, strength, mental acuity, and a capacity for attunement and aesthetic sensibility. These qualities exist in everyone and are nurtured in the ceremony. The sounds of chanting prayers, the food and flower offerings, the sweet smoke—every part of the ambiance—create an interaction between these qualities of generosity, courage, aesthetic sensibility, and our mind and heart. Then the qualities become ever more strongly present.

The offering we make in the havan is our individual awareness into the infinite awareness. We become the fire pit and the priest, and every word we utter is a mantra. We bring sweetness and love in our heart, and we are offering this sweetness and love into the Life process that we are so that this process can grow on its own, expand, become powerful, and be the energy field in which we live. The point of the havan is not, "Please, God, give me this or that." The havan is not performed to appease anyone but rather is a celebration of the abundance that we already are within and that we have around us.

During the havan, a ritual washing of the statues is performed. Milk, sugar, honey, ghee, coconut water, saffron—and if we are Kaula practitioners, alcohol—are used to wash away impurities. This has nothing to do with any notion of purity as we might think of it. In some religions, rituals are performed to purify the stain or sin that supposedly exists in all human beings. But in the spiritual practice of the havan, there is no such thing as sin; there is just the difficulty of being a human being. What is washed away in the ritual is any tension in the whole space. Impurity is tension, not sin.

Purity is not renunciation because to be truly liberated, to be free, we must be free of restriction. Purification in the havan is about becoming agenda-free, without hope for or fear of anything. Purity in spirituality is our character; it is our capacity to rise above every kind of tension and confusion, maintaining our integrity as we persevere in the cultivation of our highest potential as well as in our connections with those people with whom we share true friendship. In the havan, as in all our spiritual practice, the question of purity and impurity is one of purity of focus. This is having the ability to bring ourself completely and openly to every moment, without any other agenda than to be fully and openly there. Purity is not about eating any particular thing—or *not* eating any particular thing. During the ritual, desires that disturb our focus—which are just more tensions—are being washed out, and what remains is a special, warm feeling throughout. Having invoked that special, warm feeling, we install the forms and vibrations of the various images.

Purity in spiritual practice is about being present and open, ready and willing to participate fully and with compassion in every single moment of our life. Compassion is different from being sympathetic. Compassion means we eat our tensions, take responsibility for our life, and we do not allow ourselves to feel justified in a tension, which would only keep us from releasing it, because then we would not find within ourself the flow that is like the havan fire.

In India, this kind of event is what a person of our

spiritual practice would receive first from a teacher. They would be given a practice to do—usually without the fire, which is most often used for special occasions—and they would do it daily and then do something more elaborate twice a month, on the full and the dark of the moon.

So first the ritual is external, and then in the second level of practice, the ritual is internalized to become a visualization practice. Then, the visualization practice is distilled into a mantra repetition, because a statement about the nature of experience is being made: All experience is, at core, nothing but an energy vibration or frequency. And so this practice becomes finally the understanding that all life is Consciousness pouring Itself into Itself. And at that stage, our only practice is that of pure presence. The images of the havan—the entire havan—refer to the energy that exists in us—the power of spirit.

This ritual is about the special capacity that exists in us right now. We do not participate in a havan to absorb Indian culture, which is wonderful and fascinating but not why we do this. The havan is not about anything we are not already, or have to acquire. It is not even about acquiring enlightenment. It is Self-recognition, the recognition of what we already are—the becoming ever more deeply our Self, which transcends every culture.

In the havan, we offer our individual awareness into the infinite awareness. But we cannot enter into the awareness of infinite creative power without recognizing the infinite interdependency of all living beings while bringing to that awareness the love at the core of all manifest Life. In the havan, we are respecting that love and calling forth its fullness for every human being.

That love, which is the power of spirit, is not as much a part of us as we are of it. It is vast, huge, and unimaginable, and this body and mind are just the tiniest—ever so tiniest—tip of it. When we look into ourself more deeply, we find it there. Beyond our struggles and layers of tension in this life, we find within us a potential trying to manifest itself. We find a potency the boundaries of which we cannot discover. And it is to the manifestation of that potency that the havan, and all authentic spiritual practice, is dedicated.

WE ARE HERE TO BURN

"So the great possibility in this life is to understand...what Life Itself is....to do this, we have to be dedicated to our spiritual work and burn up the tensions that obscure the creative power within us."

IF YOU ASK ME WHY I AM HERE, I say it is to know and unfold the highest potential, the highest power, within me—or rather to allow it to unfold itself in the entire field of my awareness. For this, I do not need a relationship, career, or money. I do not even need to be healthy or particularly sane. The highest potential is unfolding me, you, us, the whole world, no matter what the circumstance of our physical existence.

To establish ourself in that highest potential, we have to burn; so we are here to burn—burn up the tensions that obscure the creative potential within us. We are here to burn up the tensions and resistance that continue to dominate our life, making that life ordinary and mundane. We are here to burn up those patterns that turn our hearts and minds towards entanglements that deny us the chance to unfold that highest power. The unfoldment of that highest power is pure joy, and if we have to burn somewhat to live within and from that joy, it is fine.

If we stay the same, how can anything special ever come into our life? And if we are going to change, then we are going to burn. We cannot be afraid of burning; we are here to take in everything and bring ourselves up to the level of the energy of that highest potential within us. In this way, every moment, we are living from and expressing in our life that highest potential.

That any of us has the chance to change deeply is wonderful, so we do not want to let that chance slip away. We have to remember: Life is not about having this or that; it is about finding the joy in our hearts. As the joy unfolds, this person and that opportunity may walk into our life, and some of that may be appealing; but most often, it is a distraction, a manifestation of a particular level that is limited; joy attracts everything. So we need to be a little careful about the choices we make. Nityananda never earned a nickel; he just made them out of thin air. He never had a job or a companion. He was not healthy; he had arthritis, liver disease, and who knows what else. And he was a saint.

So the first thing we are here to do is to get over worldly distractions and the thought that we need any thing, and that is not easy. Everybody has desires, and we are not here to deny those, to cut off, suppress, or repress them. We are here to do the work of growing and to get above the distractions, but not in some self-righteous way. We are here to burn through the tensions of desire and feel some joy in ourself and by doing this, to live in a different environment. From that environment of joy, we can begin to have a vision of how to express ourself and expand the environment in which our highest potential can unfold. Then, whatever that highest potential brings us that is of genuine benefit to our life is fine.

From desire, we cannot succeed in any creative endeavor, which takes vision—one we have experienced because we have risen above the tensions of our ordinary life. Then we transcend even the vision and go into another domain, which is how the energy itself works. And in an environment which even transcends joy and is completely peaceful, we have the understanding of the way in which experience itself arises and subsides, and how it takes shape. In my teacher's writings during the last period of his life, we see a person who mastered the energy itself. Rudi did this in a state of stillness, which means not being agitated by anything, especially burning. He used to say that this world is the Bellevue of the Solar System; everybody in it is quite mad. Some people walk around saying that *they* are not mad, creating conventions of sanity and calling them "culture"; these people want to define what "normal" is. But we have to free ourselves from such notions as normal because what we want to be is our Self.

We live in a special community full of physical beauty and talented, thoughtful people; and yet that is only part of why we are here. This community is the effect of difficult work carefully done; it represents real dedication and love. The environment is something we can drink into ourselves and benefit from deeply. This is not a place to which we come a few times a week to drop our tensions; rather, we are a part of, are nourished by, and give back to it. This becomes the vibration we live from, and wherever we go, this is the level of quality we manifest. And yet this, too, is not exactly why we are here.

This place is not about getting well; no one gets well— physically, everything is headed in one direction only. But it is about being well, which means rising above the part of ourselves that decays in order to live in a place from within that never decays. And this *is* why we are here. All our relationships are dissolved at the moment of our departure from this world, and we cannot take anything with us. So the great possibility in this life is to understand—truly to understand—what Life Itself is. That is why we are here. We have to go beyond science to the ultimate laboratory, which is our own heart and soul. And to do this, we have to be dedicated to our spiritual work and burn up the tensions that obscure the creative power within us.

That power is the place beyond decay, and we are here to live from that. From that place, miracles happen, and the ultimate miracle is that we have the chance to understand how the energy of Life operates. Then, the state of complete peace and total vastness that we are, we at last realize to be *all* that we are.

PERFECT CLARITY

"When we empty ourself of ourselves, we are in a state of clarity. This emptiness is not devoid of essence. It is an emptiness that shines; it is a clarity that is bright; its main quality is extraordinary beauty—joy."

W HEN THE BUDDHISTS TALK about emptiness, they are talking about the basis of mind, which is vast and empty of all conception—it is perfectly clear. This means it is free of any notions such as, "I am happy, sad, hungry, sore, cold, hot—I am anything." When we empty our mind of everything—of confusion or certainty, of emotional distress or emotional highs, of physical discomfort or physical vanity—and become quiet, we find that we are much bigger than our body and mind.

We are much bigger than our mind's endless capacity to limit the moment.

Our goal is to be the most loving, kind, giving, compassionate person we can be, irrespective of the circumstances about which our body or mind complains. When we can rise above our body and the resistance, the fear—whatever is in our mind—to be in touch with the potential within ourself for giving, and then put that in motion, the power in us that can serve the whole of humanity awakens. That awakening also establishes us in the highest state of perfect clarity.

Clarity unifies samsara and nirvana, hell and heaven, bringing the whole of life together and allowing us to experience our contact with that wholeness, that profound well-being that is the power of spirit. From this clarity, we see that there is no amount of penance that is going to take away a sin we do not have. There is no atonement we can do—there is no point in thinking like that at all. When we empty ourself of ourselves, we are in a state of clarity. This emptiness is not devoid of essence. It is an emptiness that shines; it is a clarity that is bright; its main quality is extraordinary beauty—joy. It is both simple and profound.

When we take hold of this clarity every single day and live from it, we can extend it so that the life we lead is not a life that is constantly assaulting our sensibility and robbing us of joy. Then we have a life in which that clarity shines out and touches the lives of all the people we meet. A transformation takes place in which the suffering around us is being released and converted into potential for ever-expanding clarity.

In the teachings of Padmasambhava, who helped to bring Buddhism to Tibet in the 8th century, as well as in the traditional practices and teachings of the culture of India, avoiding people and circumstances that give rise to disturbing emotions is believed to be the way in which clarity is cultivated and sustained. But in our culture, we have to do it a bit differently. We realize our circumstance is that we are in the world, but we understand that a calm and clear balance is appropriate to sustaining our credibility and the quality of our effort in whatever we do. And so we make sure, especially on days we might be agitated, that we spend extra time authentically doing our practice instead of using our practice to empower our worldly program.

The more the creative energy within us, the spirit within us, unfolds and expands, the greater our clarity. Confusion ceases, dissatisfaction dissolves. New desires, which come up endlessly one after the other, stop chewing at us. The expansion of spirit that comes with spiritual practice expands the joy in us and clears our heads. We are not thinking, "I want this thing; where did that thing go?" We are thinking, "What a wonderful moment," "What a fabulous day," "What wonderful people with whom to share our lives." We are chanting, praying, bowing, offering flowers and thinking, "What a beautiful Life." Our whole attitude changes, and as we are increasingly stabilized in this state—which is the state in which the Mahasiddhas consistently dwell, a state in which there is no insecurity, dissatisfaction, defensiveness—we can be perfectly clear and present in this and every time frame.

Secret Tantric practices and other early religious traditions came from the same feeling that makes people long for relationships. There is the potential within these situations to have an intense, intimate, personal, extraordinary experience that engages the whole of our biochemistry in a transcendent moment. Time is dissolved, clarity emerges—if only for a minute—because of the intensity of the focus of our energy. Unlike most relationships, though, these Tantric practices were not viewed as ends in themselves but were opportunities to create a window for the practitioner into a fine, powerful, high—a transformed—state.

Clarity is the opposite of confusion, but it is not the same as certainty, any more than it is synonymous with arrogance. This is an important distinction. Religious traditions embrace certainty. Spiritual practice is about clarity. Most religious cultures want to eliminate confusion by replacing it with certainty. These religious traditions seem at some point to have decided that confusion is worse than delusion: It is better to be misinformed and certain than it is to be totally informed and confused by it. But this certainty is based on rigidity and arrogance. It is unable to bend and change in relationship to the amount of change in the environment, and so it has a suppressive effect, which can lead to a violence born of fear.

We have to have the courage to change. This cannot be emphasized too much: A large part of spiritual practice is building confidence within ourselves so that we can live in clarity without any kind of wavering. Fear is the big issue for most people. A state of contact with the Ultimate Reality is unimaginably powerful. It releases, from within this field that we are, a forceful wave of energy that may at first disturb us profoundly. Then, instead of recognizing this powerful wave as a part of us that has just awakened and is expressing itself, we may become startled and react, taking that wave and trying to structure it. This impossible structuring creates more fear, not less, and we are back on a downward cycle.

Our meditation practice and the spiritual practices of the founders of many traditions are intended to create in us over time a depth of confidence that allows us to remain in a state of complete clarity without having our minds or hearts waver because of fear. These traditions intend to create an environment within and around us in which a clarity that comes from fulfillment and the power of spirit is present throughout the entire field of our existence. Then there is no desire or confusion, and in our embrace of change, uncertainty is no longer frightening. Instead, it is the miracle of an elegant and gracious articulation of the creative energy.

Perfect clarity is the goal of most spiritual practices. It is

~

a state of being that transcends the comings and goings of the human brain, of our desires and fears and hopes, of all our tensions. It is not to be confused with certitude, which only creates the illusion of clarity in the midst of the reality of insecurity. Perfect clarity is a stable state of total well-being in which we are centered within our Self and completely aware of the totality of the love of God, which is in fact the whole of our sensory experience. But clarity is not going to happen just because we are sitting, dwelling on it. In one ancient text that contains a training sequence for students, the point of the training practice is not meditation itself—not this practice or that practice—it is not any practice whatsoever. The effort is not in this direction or that direction; it is simply, and profoundly, to access and then live in a state of inner balance and perfect clarity.

We have to take hold of it. Clarity begins with commitment. That is taking hold of clarity: "I'm committed." This may sound coarse, but it is not, and it is important. When we are in the world, constantly bombarded by so many choices, we have to have a commitment. When we are being told that buying this product or that product is going to make us better people, we have to have a clear frame of reference that enables us every day, in the midst of this illusion, to know exactly what we are about and who we are.

If we persevere in our commitment, it stirs and becomes stronger and more powerful. It becomes devotion—because commitment is the beginning, but just that is not enough. It is a bit dry and hard. A commitment that is living, growing, that is tender, responsive, flexible, warm, yet intense and powerful, that is devotion. That devotion, kept alive and breathing, nurtured, cultivated, and expanded, rises up further. That devotion becomes a living event within each of us, which matures as a state of simple, luminous clarity—of divine love.

YOGA

~~~~

"In yoga, we use the lever that powers us in our external

pursuits...to turn our attention inside, by calling upon desire

and focusing desire on itself.... We rely on the power of the

creative energy within us, and we do not worry. This is the

ultimate detachment."

THE PRACTICE OF YOGA IN ALL
its forms is about a deeply personal, individual experience,
a deeply personal vision of God. Through yoga, we strive
to experience and sustain this vision. Spiritual growth is
about having the strength to sustain the vision as we move
through our everyday life. Often we hear that we should
divorce ourselves from all material circumstances; this is

talked about as renunciation or detachment. However, among the people who practice kundalini yoga, there is a different view. For them, the practice of yoga is not about detachment—it is not about material things—because there is only one thing in the whole universe; material things are no more or less pure than nonmaterial anything. To the practitioners of kundalini yoga, we should not think about attachment and detachment but rather live from the fullness, the abundance, the effulgence, the overflowing creative energy of Life.

In the context of living from that fullness, we allow everything to flow so that there is no entanglement in any external circumstance. We are not chasing anything nor are we averse to anything. We allow our life to happen as it wants to happen. Rather than thinking about material circumstances or any kind of philosophical issues related to renunciation, attachment, and detachment, we become established in the fullness of the creative power within us. From the attunement to that creative power, which yoga promotes, our vision of God will naturally unfold from within, as our own essence reveals its extraordinary vastness to our mind, senses, and body. Then we are at peace.

~

Established in that awareness, the past suddenly has no relevance. What meaning can the past have in the context of growing into and becoming part of the infinite? To be established in the awareness of that infinite creative power is to let the past go completely—to let go of the things we think we want and do not want, the things we used to want and not want. The miracle is to live from that Life that the highest creative power within us is trying to deliver for us from within ourself. When we are tangled up in the past, there is a profound restriction on the flow of that creative power.

Only when we rise above the past and what we hope for the future do we have the possibility of seeing beyond our ego and desires—Shaiva pundits say we see the world the way we are—to see the world and ourself with infinite vision. Then the term "commitment," which seems to imply some kind of attachment, takes on a different meaning. Commitment becomes our stable connection to, our stable experience of that highest creative power, which is trying to deliver from within us an extraordinary vision, flavor, resonance, a symphony of miracles that are the demonstration of that power, which is the source of the whole universe. The power that created the whole universe is within each of us.

Commitment, then, is not about a thing, a place, or a belief system; it is commitment to a vision, a state. Commitment then means relying on that state as we move through the world and experience the fear, uncertainty, struggle, pain that go with walking around in a physical body in this physical existence. Our commitment is to the highest teacher and the highest teaching that dwells deeply, silently, subtly within us—not in relationship to any place in our physical body but subtly within the presence that we are. It is to that presence that we should be attached and in that presence that we should be established all the time. Then the ups and downs of our material, physical, emotional, individual life are nothing more than that highest creative power trying to unwrap the patterns of tension and trauma we have accumulated so that something profound can pour through the layers.

One of the reasons we have a physical teacher in our life is as a reality check. When tensions release—and buried desires, circumstances, and deep obstructions come up—the teacher helps us *not* to become entangled in the illusions that are part of the release. That same presence that has called forth from within us a vision of ultimate reality functions as a support to the unfoldment of that reality. The teacher helps us to find the harmony and alignment with that reality as we strive to experience the vision and manifest it in our physical life.

This flow with that power within ourself does not cause us to make tense gestures and tight facial expressions. We use the term "work" because we have great respect for the amount of concentration and energy required to shift our state from that of an individual, limited person struggling in the world with delusion to a person who is established in the vision of their own infinite creative power, experiencing the joy and peace that are the qualities of that creative power. We do not use the term "work" to denote tension.

Asanas, or postures, in yoga are not mental postures. These are physical postures that keep the energy in the body in order to keep the body healthy while we spend long periods in meditation. These asanas are not about self-improvement or any self-absorbing notion that causes more mental tension. This is a work that compels us to stop the struggle, release the tensions, adjust our frame of reference so that we remember: This is about love, not judgment; flow, not tension; there are no grades. The work might be harder than we thought because it is much more subtle than we imagined; it is about real flow, real love.

In yoga practice, we do have some behavioral routines, but they are not about gaining God's favor. God has given us the power to create our own heaven or our own hell, and also the responsibility for living in whatever it is we do. All behavioral programs in yoga come down to this: respect and love for everybody.

True love does not come today and go tomorrow. It comes and stays through every kind of difficulty and uncertainty. It transcends giving and getting, coming and going, up and down. It is a presence in our life that brings stability and allows us at the same time to have the freedom to transcend ourselves continuously. Then we do not think about what we want and do not want, need and do not need, like and dislike, or any other dichotomy and duality. We think about how to love our life and the people in it. We practice that, and that is the practice of yoga.

Yoga is about loving our life, about growing within our

greater Life. It is about the ability to feel literally our spirit and to feel that spirit all the time, under every circumstance—to allow that spirit, that strength, to be nourished and grow stronger. In the pursuit of a worldly life, most of our energy is turned outside towards the achievement of some objective. But in yoga, the longing to grow spiritually turns this energy inside, towards reorganizing ourself. Then we no longer operate on a narrow band of perception, limited by the range of our desires. We begin to live from the experience of spirit, which is intimately connected with the source of the whole of Life—which is the vitality of this unbroken, infinite, reciprocally interrelated, dynamic system that has as its second quality pure consciousness, pure awareness. Its first quality is total freedom.

In yoga, we use the lever that powers us in our external pursuits to begin to turn our attention inside, by calling upon desire and focusing desire on itself. Thus, we ultimately transcend desire but do not suppress it. Transforming desire and transcending desire are the essence of any spiritual practice. In this way, we unfold all the profound possibilities hidden within us and allow everyone around us to manifest those same possibilities within themselves.

We rely on the power of the creative energy within us, and we do not worry. This is the ultimate detachment. It is not that we turn our backs on the world—that is basically impossible. Even the most reclusive spiritual practitioners living in the Himalayas require people to bring them food.

We rely on the creative power within. Great yogis do not have to turn their backs on the world or on material things. Authentic students of spiritual work depend on the power of the creative energy always. They understand deeply from within themselves the appropriate pathway that is in front of them, and they put their foot on it every single day with respect for life and with love for everyone whom they meet on the way. Through the practice of yoga, we have that deeply sacred and profound, personal experience of God that has been the essence of mystical traditions since the beginning of time.

SPIRITUAL PRACTICE IS
OUR DAILY LIFE

"...a person devoted to a spiritual practice, down to and up to the infinite degree of their personal resource, is attempting to establish themselves in the highest state of flow, which manifests first as compassion for themselves and then as love and respect for all human beings."

MEDITATION IS WHAT ALL OF us can do immediately to change our life. In meditation, we are reaching through the tension, struggles, issues, thoughts, feelings, ups and downs of daily living; we are reaching through the many to the one place from which our life draws its innate power. In simply connecting to that place, even for a little while, our life becomes richer.

In time, as we are able to sustain that connection longer, the richness that unfolds from within us is, for the most part, unimaginable by people; the beauty, joy, happiness, and quality of life experience possible are rarely discovered by people.

The possibilities within may often be unimaginable, but through meditation practice, they are realizable. Take a little while and be aware of that extraordinary experience of life pulsating within, and with the awareness of the breath, allow that experience to expand and grow. This practice of tuning into the breath is fundamentally important, not just when we are sitting but also, and especially, when we are not, when we are faced with the difficulties of daily life.

Each person has to choose the form of their life. We are not completely free, on a personal level, to be anything we may want because the world is limited in terms of physical resources. But the potential within everyone, which is the energetic resource, is not limited at all. Only when we dedicate ourself to spiritual growth do we have the chance to tap into that resource, which is the fundamental power of Life Itself—the power of spirit that animates our bodies and

~

minds and is the source of joy and satisfaction in our experience. The term for the expansion of that infinite resource within is the awakening of kundalini, or kundalini yoga.

At a certain point, not long into the practice of meditation, we notice a rhythm to the sequence of experiences as we sit, and we may also notice ourselves becoming uncomfortable. That discomfort is the resistance intrinsic to any state as a transition takes place. These resistances are dealt with by simply breathing, feeling, extending our awareness through them, not by reacting to them. This is true when we are dealing with resistance in ourselves, in anyone, any resistance that develops in our life as our life becomes patterned—and everybody's life becomes patterned. But we try not to react to the resistance, and this is a big part of what meditation training is. We are training ourselves not to react to any of the resistances we encounter within ourselves or other people with whom we work.

And the flip side of that is, we are always promoting, facilitating, cultivating a flow. The basic change of state we are trying to bring about in cultivating a flow within ourself is from disappointment to fulfillment. From being a disappointed person to being a fulfilled person. This is what the Tantric tradition and kundalini yoga, and ultimately all spirituality, are about—promoting this change of state. We understand, from that flow within ourself, that our fulfillment is not in the slightest dependent on anything outside us, on anything outside that flow within. We are promoting that flow within in order to discover that state of fulfillment already present within us. In staying open to other human beings at all times and promoting a flow—not reacting to resistance, our own or anyone else's—we are expanding and reinforcing that happiness within ourself and sharing it with those people with whom we share our life. Then, the more we grow, the more our family becomes the whole of humanity.

Meditation practice is about this contact with flow; yoga is about this flow—the asanas or postures in yoga facilitate flow, which is the power of spirit. The first step toward opening our hearts to that power within—in our spiritual practice, in the whole of our life—is simply to bring our attention inside and become aware of our breath and with our breath, to relax our body, to start to feel the flow within. Then we are releasing tension and allowing energy to flow and expand in us. Our breath will take us inside always.

~

Focusing on, establishing, and sustaining the flow mean we have to be willing to give of ourself, in the moment, whatever is necessary, with the hope that at some point, an equilibrium in our relationships will be established, and there will be a sharing, a give-back, with which we can build. If there is not, then we may have to pull back a bit until an equilibrium *is* established. Ultimately, though, any real relationship is based, not on receiving, but on giving. Self-sacrifice will of course constrain our behavior, but the underlying phenomenon we are focusing on—the power of spirit—is in fact unconstrained, and at various points, changes of state do take place that facilitate a dissolution of restraint and an expansion of the whole system.

So we respond to difficulties in our everyday life based on our training, and we participate in a subtle way that allows for expansion. The real focus has to be constantly on our practice, and we are concerned with the circulation of the energy within ourself as a mechanism for distributing change. If we do this work, then the whole universe will reorganize itself around and in support of it. Like a strange attractor in the scientific discussion of chaos—a strange attractor is a stillpoint in a dynamic pattern—when we become a stillpoint, then the reorganization of the life patterns around us is the same as the descent of grace. And it is a self-reinforcing mechanism: Change outside promotes change inside, and it feeds on itself, expands, and becomes a self-sustaining, dynamic event. This self-sustaining, dynamic event we ignite within ourself.

Mystics call this the fire of love, not a personal fire of personal love, but a personal fire of transcendent love—love of Life Itself. It allows for a total reordering of our environment. It is a mechanism by which we become released from our individual limitations, our limited perspective—released from all levels. In this environment of expansion, the potentiality hidden in every human being becomes liberated.

There is a rhythm to our internal experience of this liberation, a rhythm to our relationships with one another. There is a rhythm in and to everything, of which we can be aware, and in being aware of these rhythms, we can be in harmony with them. We can maintain our center and focus and not develop false expectations or have unfortunate reactions.

~

For example, what if someone says something hurtful and our hearts close, and we begin to get upset? If we have been practicing, our training kicks in—we bring our focus down, bring the energy down, our minds become quiet, and although our hearts are still a bit hard, our breathing starts to stabilize. That change becomes distributed throughout our systems. We bring the energy up again. We are breathing. This process allows us to establish some refined interaction with a difficult situation, and then we see it for what it really is. The offense we were about to take and leave forever was unnecessary because there was a way for us to handle our part of the event that came from a deeper place within us and contacted a deeper place— that same place—within everyone else.

It is difficult to unhurt someone's feelings after they have been hurt. We can work through and reopen the channels within ourself because we have that understanding, but if we damage the connection between ourself and somebody else in a moment of intense emotional distress, it may never become undamaged because that takes mutual cooperation in an environment in which there is now trauma. That is not easy.

It takes consciously disciplining ourselves and creating a flow first within us and then within our circumstance in the world to be able to cut through potential dissonance—or actual dissonance—to have a deeper understanding, and in that deeper understanding, to allow for a deeper rapport and change of state to take place. When we feel tension or agitation, we have to focus on what we focus on in any and all states: the breath. Then our superficial emotions do not matter; there is an endless flow. It is the nature of the world that oceans evaporate and become gas that condenses over land, falls to earth, and becomes rain—or in wintertime in cold places, meltable ice and snow—which is water that flows to the ocean and evaporates; there is an endless flow, endless flow. So if we focus on that part of us, the simplest part—the breath—which is endlessly flowing, and we pay attention to that tide, then all the cycles of change of state will suddenly reveal themselves to us as a total unity. Then there is no thought about tension and agitation, about what this or that is. Everything is one thing.

Agitation is just a different frequency of energy in operation, and we want to absorb it as much as we can into our own system so that it becomes productive for us. New experiences are intrinsically disturbing, and this is wonderful. So we are quiet and take as much time as necessary to digest and absorb new experiences and to reflect upon them in a thoughtful way. Even if it is an experience that is never recreated and we never go back to it, for whatever reason, we can always benefit. We can benefit from pleasant experiences; we can benefit from painful, unhappy experiences. The point is not to add up the sum total of the painful and pleasurable experiences because in life, these things do not add up.

Life is painful. But by taking the benefit from every experience, we transcend the discussion of pleasure and pain and have a life that is fulfilling, infinitely expanding, truly alive. Then we consume and transcend all emotional states as an expression of self-discipline, because if we are susceptible to various changes in our emotional state, we are going to make some profound mistakes that will not benefit us or the people who are dear to us. We have to breathe through it. We have to train ourselves to respond to our emotional states by closing our mouth, because that is our most dangerous weapon—or most powerful tool.

Then we become aware of our breathing, focusing our attention on our bellies and circulating the energy, allowing for the emotional state to be distributed throughout our systems.

And then we understand one thing clearly: Ninety-nine percent of the pain we experience in our life has its origin in us. And a person who cannot take responsibility for their own life cannot grow. If my teacher, Rudi, trained those of us who were with him to anything, it was to face every circumstance life brought us with the single-minded determination to grow. Then nothing is that person's fault over there; it is not about anyone but us. If we are focused on changing our own patterns, then so many patterns around us will change naturally. We do our part; that is the only part we can do.

We must not expect human beings to be something different from human beings. Along with everyone else, we, too, can do the whole human dance. We can be happy, sad, comforting, hurt, angry, wrong, right. The whole dance. But it would be wise not to get "into" it, not to invest any emotional currency or any of our integrity in the dance. It is just the dance of life. And just because

~

someone is a dedicated spiritual student does not mean they are "right" or holier than anybody else. It does not mean there is such a thing as "right." What it does mean is that a person devoted to a spiritual practice, down to and up to the infinite degree of their personal resource, is attempting to establish themselves in the highest state of flow, which manifests first as compassion for themselves and then as love and respect for all human beings.

To establish ourself in and to sustain that state of flow, we manage our emotions. We have something within us that is complete and perfect as it is. The degree to which we can reel in our mind and emotions, centering our awareness in the power of spirit, allowing its creative potentiality to flow in and from us, is the degree to which we can release that potentiality. Our real practice begins in the moments when we are not struggling anymore; we have to rise above the struggle and become peaceful. Whatever demons hassle us, we give them a hug and kiss, and send them on their way. Then we sit down and are at ease; we do not bring those demons with us.

It is fine to have success in our worldly life, but that success is often at the expense of the highest state of spiritual potential that exists within us. So it is up to us. It is exciting to sit quietly and observe the fluctuation of Life Itself within us, revealing its power from the deepest, quiet place within the ultimate reality of this life and the whole universe. This excitement is an infinite excitement; its endurance transcends time and space. Other excitements come and go only too quickly. But we do have to be respectful of the productive effects of sitting quietly in the infinite. We want to reinvest continually in spiritual work; as in any endeavor, many people are sidetracked by the first benefits.

Our breathing exercises, everything in our spiritual practice, are about coming to a point where we are at peace. Our basic practice is to learn to relax and flow within ourself. It is to learn to open to all the different circumstances that present themselves to us and to flow in them, rather than reacting against and resisting the change they may represent. The power of Life Itself is so profoundly wise that it endlessly presents circumstances that are that power organizing itself in a reciprocal balanced interchange with patterns of tension for the purpose of release, resolution, and unfoldment. Encouraging this wisdom to express itself in our daily life is the focus of the true student of spiritual practice.

THE TEACHER AND OUR
OWN HUMANITY

~~~

"Inspired by a living teacher, we find that place in us beyond

tension, beyond any daily struggles, and we believe in it, trust

and love it, nurture and grow it—we find that power of spirit,

which is authentic love, within us."

IT IS IMPORTANT THAT OUR
teacher be a human and living teacher. This is in contrast
to the idea that a teacher can be someone who has passed
from this existence or who has never been alive. Such teachers may just be an idealization we can manipulate—our
notion of perfect qualifications—rather than a living event
that prompts us to grow. There is perfection inherent in

~

everything, and part of that perfection is the uniqueness of every diverse manifestation of it.

To have a human teacher is truly to learn how to love— to really love somebody—because we may not, and probably will not, fully understand our teacher. We will have uncertainties about every aspect of the interaction. And learning to love someone deeply, completely, and genuinely is to find in that person a flow and a value that allow us to come back always to a fundamental stillpoint, a connectedness between ourself and the teacher. This connectedness makes it possible for what is truly valuable to be present and experienced. Then we can build from that.

In thirty years of being a teacher, I have found throughout the world profoundly special people, but I would not describe them as perfect. The idea of relating to perfection is in some sense a denial. If we are relating to something perfect from our own imperfection, it makes the perfection inaccessible.

The point of having a human teacher is to learn to love enough that we can love ourself. And that means it is okay to be a bit weird. Everybody is a bit weird. *Everybody*. And we have to have an environment in which there is enough love that it is okay for that weirdness to come out and off-gas—not a touchy-feely environment but real caring that is there when we need it. This caring may not always be evident, but when we need it, it is there. We can be who we are; we can let tensions fall out of us, and it is alright. There are two kinds of religion: the religion of laws and the religion of love. In the religion of love, profound toler-ance, acceptance, and caring allow us to transcend the ten-sions in one another and to find in the idiosyncrasies of each other and of this world something of authentic mean-ing and value.

To have the company of accomplished people is the most extraordinary opportunity, and we have to step up to it. We have to find from within ourself some way to par-ticipate in the specialness of the accomplishment of people like my teacher, Rudi, and his teacher, Nityananda. The Buddhist saint Milarepa, at the behest of his teacher, Marpa, spent twelve years building, tearing down, and rebuilding the same structure, in order to receive just the first level of oral instruction. Twelve years of hard labor with no posi-tive feedback, in order to generate an interaction with a person of Marpa's rare capacity—it was, and is, worth it.

In the Buddhist and Hindu Tantras, the three main things to be cherished are the teacher, the practice, and the spiritual community; three things in life are truly worthwhile: the teacher, absorbing what the teacher is transmitting, and fine people with whom to share the experience. These are the three jewels of Buddhism, but they are beyond any one tradition because they are about authentic love. The teacher is about authentic love. At the most basic level of the energetic structure of our meditation class, the teacher takes on the suffering of other people; this requires true love and a great deal of strength, and it is the ultimate act of sacrifice. Dealing with the confusion of people—living with their lack of peace and their doubts about themselves, which are often dumped upon the teacher—is an act of great compassion.

As we grow, we are striving to achieve our own complete release from this cycle of existence, and we may increasingly just naturally withdraw from the company of human beings, establishing ourself in an undisturbed state of perfect clarity. But the teacher sacrifices by doing the additional work of living among human beings, who are inherently disturbing. The teacher makes the effort necessary to sustain clarity in that disturbed environment and to help others find that clarity within themselves; the teacher takes great risks.

Living in this world causes confusion for most people. Many people want to grow, but the confusion they experience causes them to retreat from the possibility of real growth—to retreat from their own creative energy, which is the power of spirit working within them—and to fall into a state of profound self-doubt. A great deal of energy is necessary to free someone from this, but tensions sap individual energy resources. The teacher is the energy source that allows people to connect to that part within that can and will grow. And so it is important to keep faith with the special connection with the teacher, no matter what.

Most people have no idea of the cost to the teacher of bringing that extraordinary energy, that powerful love, to the student. The teacher takes on the tensions, poisons, sicknesses—both physical and emotional—of the student and burns them up. It is a sacrifice of the teacher's energy and of the teacher's body for the benefit of the student. So as we are compassionate with ourselves regarding our own humanity, we are also compassionate with the teacher and grateful for their humanity: If they were not human, they would not be here, and then where would we be?

Strictly speaking, the teacher does not "teach" us anything. Spirituality is not something that can be taught, although it can be learned. In this learning process, we need a guide, a mentor. The Sanskrit word for teacher is "guru," which does not mean teacher of lessons but rather dispeller of darkness. The distinction is important: A spiritual teacher is necessary, not to bring us anything outside that we do not already have, but to uncover in us the power of spirit that lies buried beneath the darkness of our tensions. These tensions come from the choices we make precisely because we think that something outside is needed for us to be happy.

Whenever we come to a teacher, it is wise to forget about anything we think we know and instead to bring ourselves to baseline, ground zero. Then we have the possibility of real benefit from an authentic learning experience. Ultimately, this is a practice we want to have with everybody—we want to come to ground zero with every human being so that we have a chance to interact

~

authentically with them, free of any veil of assumptions and egotism.

We do not think about approval or disapproval where the teacher is concerned. Nobody judges us except ourselves. We judge ourselves when we create tensions that complicate our life and deny us the possibility of bringing forth the finest qualities—the most refined, subtle, sensitive, sophisticated qualities—of heart, mind, and action that are present deep within us.

In spiritual texts, when practitioners talk about pleasing the guru, they mean finding that place within that is peaceful and flowing and from that peaceful and open place, discovering the point of contact—reaching from and feeling from it. If we reach with our minds, we miss it. We find that subtle point of contact deep within ourself, and then we breathe into it, allowing a true communion to take place. We do that and do that and do that, bringing that experience more and more into our everyday life as we encounter all kinds of diverse people and events.

Inspired by a living teacher, we find that place in us beyond tension, beyond any daily struggles, and we believe in it, trust and love it, nurture and grow it—we find that power of spirit, which is authentic love, within us. Then we hold onto that love through all the confusion, suffering, and everything the world throws at us. We hold to that specialness, which is the infinite loving presence of God, and in growing that presence in ourself, we transcend confusion, suffering, tension, and brutality to arrive at a perfectly clear and completely loving place.

It was wonderful to have access to my teacher, Rudi, Swami Rudrananda. He was sweet, loving, kind, caring, but his company was not free. I do not mean this in any monetary sense, but in the finest and highest sense: We did not just waltz in and "hang" with Rudi. We worked deeply inside ourself and physically very hard, morning, noon, and night, seven days a week, twenty-four hours a day. It was intense.

Rudi was a phenomenon and a paradox; he transcended himself and was not an individual anymore. He was human, but he became so open and deeply cultivated as a human being that he was more of a loving presence than a person. That loving presence was not a comforting presence all the time because that powerful love was regularly disturbing the attempt to establish some kind of order that

⌒

all people try in vain to make. Rudi was a volcano, and the connection to that profound fire of love transformed us completely.

Rudi was about love and flow. He was friends with every kind of person and had the ability to have meaningful interaction with anyone he encountered. In being about flow, he was continually reaching through the form of anybody—not judging, not making up his mind, "This is a person I can exchange with; this is a person I can't." He was constantly finding the love within himself and finding love in everybody and everything. He did whatever was appropriate—taking on appropriate body language or speech—to allow for real communication.

Great people we have the chance to meet in our life may bust our butt—and in the process, we discover two important things. One is that we can do the work—we *are able* to do it. The other is that we learn to love and respect other people who may seem profoundly different from us. We learn that everything and everyone has the same source.

Rudi did not always look like the idea someone might have of a spiritual teacher. His dress was not out of the

ordinary much of the time; he was not a vegetarian all of
the time. His example taught us that this work is not about
anything looking like what we expect. It is not about looking pretty or saintly; it is about growing. We are not here
to be perfect—or normal, whatever that is—we are here
to grow. We are here to grow in accord with the power of
spirit within us, in whatever way that power chooses to
manifest in us. Spiritual growth is not about what we want;
it is about what the power within us wants for us.

To make the connection to a living teacher, we have to
develop the capacity to keep our heart open all the time,
no matter what anything does or does not look like. We
are continuously taking our energy, fortified by the loving
energy of the teacher, and reinforcing within ourself a state
of openness that allows generations of tensions, poisons,
limitations to fall out of us and burn away. This liberates
capability in us; it liberates strengths, energies in us of which
we are not aware.

Traditionally, when people are concerned about purity—
about perfection and not being human—they are actually
concerned about the accumulation and conservation of
power. But power that does not flow is the source of an

hypocrisy that poisons people. The focus has to be on flow and opening our hearts and being compassionate towards other human beings as well as towards ourselves.

Anytime we undertake an authentic spiritual practice, it is impossible to be anything other than a human being. There is no doctrine, no dogma that can contain the dimensions of creative power that unfold from authentic spiritual practice and no box in which to put an authentic practitioner. I think of Rudi as a Mahasiddha. That is a term that speaks to the reality of people who are beyond any religion, who are powerful, authentic people—the most authentic—and they live beyond every kind of classification.

Rudi taught us that true love exists within every person, regardless of outward appearance. The power of spirit exists within every person. There is no other. And it is our responsibility to excavate that true love, that power of spirit, from our layers of tension, compression, egotism, arrogance, complexity, and fear. This is the work of an authentic spiritual life. Rudi taught us that true love is something that takes commitment, dedication, and sacrifice.

So following the example of the teacher, we are forgiving of everyone because life is not easy and all human beings suffer. Our spiritual work is about loving and being loved, period, because the way we find some authentic and enduring sweetness and meaningfulness in life is in our commitment and devotion to cultivating authentic love and in our capacity to hold to it, no matter what.

ALIGNMENT

~~~

"In this alignment with the teachers, the power and knowledge in the teachers flow down on and through the practitioners. In this way, the practitioners accumulate the power to do productively the practices they are given by their living teacher."

*I*N THE MORNING, THERE IS A serious yet uncomplicated practice of spiritual alignment to be done. It has similarities to the Para Puja of the Trika in Shaivism and to the Tibetan Buddhist practice of Chöd. Like them, it is not dualistic; unlike them, it does not take place after sunset, does not contain material offerings, as in the Para Puja, or orally spoken mantras, as in both. It

~

uses visualization, as do Chöd and Para Puja, but it is the practice through which a person accumulates the empowerment to perform successfully these other practices. This meditation aligns a practitioner every day with their living teacher and the lineage that has gone before.

This morning yoga meditation begins by sitting down and visualizing the teacher, the guru, seated on a gold cushion, gold chair, or gold disk, four fingers below the navel chakra or energy center. The practitioners tune into this visualization of the guru, catching hold of its vibration. They then feel that presence of the guru, that power, that energy, rise up to their heart, which relaxes, encouraging further opening and sweetness. As that sweetness accumulates, the practitioners breathe to promote it. They feel the presence of the guru living inside them, and they bring that presence up, out the top of the head, twelve fingers above the head. At that point, the practitioners visualize their teacher's teacher coming out of the guru and then his or her teacher coming out of that guru.

The practitioners then call all the rest of the lineage together, all the Mahasiddhas and different spiritual teachers the practitioners respect, and they visualize them. In that visualization, the practitioners send their gurus love and respect, genuinely grateful for the presence of the lineage in their life. They see that the whole of the lineage is permeated with infinite space; all teachers are as big as infinite space, and infinite space is contained within the teachers. The practitioners hold this visualization for as long as possible.

Visualizing means that the practitioner is truly seeing. It is somewhat like daydreaming, where a person is free of the body yet the images are clear. But visualization is not just a daydream. Keeping the body loose and relaxed, the practitioner starts with the feeling of connection to the body, and instead of going from somewhere to somewhere else, which is the duality of daydreaming, the practitioner opens from the body into the reality of the visualization— the practitioner expands into it. In this practice, the practitioner does not go from one place to another and back again. Because the practice integrates ever more subtle energies into this infinite presence, there is no duality. There is no here; there is no there. There is only this infinite presence present.

In this alignment with the teachers, the power and

knowledge in the teachers flow down on and through the practitioners. In this way, the practitioners accumulate the power to do productively the practices they are given by their living teacher. In addition, the practitioners accumulate real power to help people. That real power is both understanding and energy; it also might be connections with people. So the proper understanding is what to do, when, and how, because it is not enough just to have an idea of such a practice. The practitioners have to understand how that idea unfolds in time and space and what the appropriate sequentiality of it is. Otherwise, the practice is useless; whatever is done turns into a muddle; the energy will not support it.

Through this daily morning practice, practitioners accumulate energy, understanding, and deep sensitivity. Through alignment, the practitioners draw upon the energy of their entire lineage, and that knowledge and power become resonant in them; they feel the connection deeply nourishing them. The lineage settles ever more profoundly in the practitioners, and they feel in their individual self, in their physical body, this connection they are honoring, which in turn nourishes, uplifts, and upholds them.

CONSECRATED ACTION

⌒

"The point of all yoga practice is to center ourself in that spirit within us, which then powers all our action and nonaction."

Whatever work there is to be done can be thought of as consecrated action. Action has several dimensions to it: ritual and physical action, mental and emotional activity, spiritual practice. In the *Bhagavad Gita*, these dimensions are discussed at length. Nonaction, which is the term for meditation in the book, is also discussed. Which is higher? Ultimately, we cannot have one without the other.

Spiritual practice becomes a discussion, then, not just of meditation practice, or nonaction, but of something else as well. That something is referred to in an ancient Shaiva text as centering techniques. Every moment of every day, whether we are meditating or not, we center ourself in the awareness of the divine creative power within us. We center our individual awareness in the infinite awareness that is the power of spirit within. In the intense centeredness that emerges is an experience of the presence of the power of spirit throughout the total field of our environment. If we are really aware, we feel it not just in our body, in the channels and chakras, or in the body around us, or in the room; we feel into the extraordinary subtlety and sophistication that we are. To feel this subtlety and multidimensionality of Life is to experience the wonder and miracle of our existence.

As we become completely quiet and center ourself in our Self, that power of spirit within us will speak to the appropriate action for us. We simply center ourself and listen; what that power says to us from day to day will not be the same. So rather than expecting that in meditation at some stage somebody is going to run through our heads and flip on light bulbs, we center ourself consistently in the infinite creative potential, the awareness within us. We move through our everyday life from that dimension of awareness, and this allows for a profound transformation within our nervous system, hearts and minds, as well as in our material existence.

Then, anyone who is sincerely on a spiritual path, anyone who is working to center in that awareness, understands that whatever misfortune happens to them in the short term in their life is a function of the highest creative power resolving from within various obstructions, limitations, and difficulties. This ultimately brings about a much finer state of awareness and level of existence. As we move through this world centered in our awareness, a confidence, a trust, in that awareness slowly builds within us, allowing us ever more deeply to relax and live an infinite, beautiful, joyous, spontaneous experience.

The point of all yoga practice is to live from the experience of spirit that is the essence of our heart and mind. It is about developing the ability to feel that spirit and hear that spirit all the time in our life, no matter what. The point of all yoga practice is to center ourself in that spirit within us, which then powers all our action and nonaction. We have to know what it is we are living for, what it is that makes life worth living, so that we can center ourself in what is enduringly uplifting, nourishing, and beautiful. Then all the work that we do is indeed consecrated action.

GETTING OVER
OURSELVES TO
GIVE OF OUR SELF

"We make our life, and we offer it for the sake of the world.

And we do it because we care about Life, because we care

about the people who have given us something special—we

care to give something back."

*H*OW NICE TO GATHER TOGETHER
and be grateful for the extraordinary richness we have in
our life. That is the point of an occasion like this, Thanksgiving Day. We are here today to be thankful, which reminds us every day to be thankful. We are gathering always
to be grateful for the extraordinary grace, the power of

spirit, that surrounds us. And this means that we are thinking about what it is to give of ourself in this life and, in whatever ways we can, to bring the best part of ourself to the moment.

If we are going to grow, it is important that we grow what we have—that we nurture, cultivate, and expand it. The wonderful thing that makes every human being special and potentially great is the possibility that exists within to connect to the power of spirit and to grow that power—to awaken to it, to open and expand it. The endeavor of releasing that power of spirit is the source of all richness that exists in everybody's life.

When we talk about richness, we are not talking about money. Money is a question of luck. Some people are smart and lucky, others are smart, work hard, and are dead broke. Money may be earned, but it is not an issue of "deserved," and it is not what makes our life rich.

What makes our life rich is our capacity to forget about ourselves, our problems—our capacity to find within ourself that special energetic power that through our conscious effort, our choice, we awaken, expand, and extend throughout the whole of our life to the people we meet every day.

Instead of getting caught up in tensions, differences, distinctions, we rise above ourselves and from within ourself contribute something of value to every interaction—even if it is just a smile. Instead of focusing on what we are getting out of an interaction, even when someone is grumbling, we keep looking to the source of that richness within us until we deeply feel the love and joy that is the power of spirit, and we extend that. Then someone else's grumbling does not matter. Our lives become infinitely rich.

In the early days of the Rudrananda Ashram, we used to spend about four dollars on dinner for everyone—not apiece, for everyone. We did not have shower stalls, so the girls walked to the physical education building on the Indiana University campus to take a shower. But we didn't care; it was all a wonderful adventure. We did not have anything material, but we had enthusiasm, a willingness to work, and we were happy. Nobody had the money to take a plane to see Rudi in New York, so we piled into a beat-up van and drove all night to see him. And this was not just true of the ashram in Indiana; it was true of the ashrams in Boston, Big Indian, Cincinnati—everywhere.

We did not think one second about what we did not

have; we only felt the whole universe was right in front of us and that God was standing behind us. We were permeated with gratitude, and we still are. So we remember to breathe Life, taste It, feel It, and enjoy—really enjoy—It because that is what Life is and growing is. They are about deeply, deeply enjoying everything and having within ourself an experience of sweetness that transcends any kind of accomplishment or possession.

Life is strange. Very few people get where they want to go, and most of the people who get there are not happy when they do. It is only when we get over ourselves and give ourself away that we can feel joy, feel it grow and expand. Then we find in life something strange, yes, and mysterious, yes, but also extraordinary and beautiful, bountiful and gracious. The power of spirit pours forth every kind of richness; the power of spirit is the essence of all enjoyment; and it is through self-sacrifice that the power of spirit unfolds.

Chöd, Indian Buddhist in its origin, is a cremation ground practice that has at its core the same type of sacrifice that all Kaulas have done since the beginning of time, and all Shaivas, and Nityananda and Rudi, and

~

Padmasambhava—all Tantric Buddhists and Hindus, it does not matter. It is the same sacrifice. It is also like the Christian practice of communion and the remembrance of Jesus in the Last Supper. It is about complete self-sacrifice—not only in order to do something profound to help someone else but also, deeply and completely, to let go within ourselves. This is so that what we worry about and doubt in ourselves and in everybody else can be released, and we can be a profoundly big, clear, open, loving person.

Realization is having a steady, clear, open mind; a perfectly clear, open heart. And then each and every moment is so full that we do not worry about what is coming next, and we do not think about what has gone before. The three times—past, present, and future—are all one time. And all the millions of various Hindu, Buddhist, and even Christian hells are purified and transformed into a present heaven, a life that is beautiful.

I like to describe the work we do as cultivating. Gardening can be difficult; cultivating is demanding; the taking of the fruits, that is fun. Many people do not love the work and can only think about the fruit. But if we love the work, the growth, the cultivating, as well as the taking of the fruit, then nothing is an obstacle to realization, and sacrifice is a natural part of the process.

Perseverance with love triumphs over every obstacle. The original people who established the holiday of Thanksgiving came from a great distance. They worked in the face of adversity and suffered tremendously—they nearly died out completely. But challenged by this tremendous uncertainty, their devotion, love, and perseverance triumphed.

The responsibility of each of us is to take what we have been given and continually add value to it, improve and enrich it—not for the sake of our own name, our own aggrandizement, but for the sake of the world. We make our life, and we offer it for the sake of the world. And we do it because we care about Life, because we care about the people who have given us something special— we care to give something back. And we do this with the understanding that many people are often confused and self-absorbed. But still, we make life wonderful, and we pray that this wonderful life that we make will genuinely benefit—whomever. We want to give back in spite of the limitations of human beings because we care about the

~

ways—whatever they may be—that Life has blessed us. We reach through the tensions, despair, difficulties to see the benefit, and we care. We do this in order to make something finer that will be absorbable by someone and thereby bring the rest of humanity even a quarter of a centimeter closer to a sweetness and joy in their own experience of being.

The quality of communication starts when we are open, joyous, willing to share. We have to get above the screwiness in ourselves to do this. We have to forget all the tensions, fears, and clinging, and connect to the joy within us, live from the joy within us, sharing every single thing we possibly can from within ourself and appreciating every interaction. If we cannot appreciate this, ultimately it is no one's tension but our own. So we appreciate the power of dedication and devotion, as well as the potential of hard work, to transform us and the entire field of our existence. But this will only happen if we give ourselves completely away. What is true love, anyway, but that kind of giving?

THE BASIS OF
SPIRITUAL GROWTH

"Spiritual growth requires commitment. We do not just practice self-sacrifice until it hurts and then call it quits.... Doing something when it is hard is when it really counts."

*T*HE BASIS OF SPIRITUAL GROWTH is the transcendence of any boundaries or limitations we think we have; this means transcending time and space. And we cannot transcend time and space and have a concern for ourselves. The Self that we wish to unfold from within us, the Self of Hindu Tantric literature, is the same emptiness aspired to in Buddhist Tantric literature. Theologians may argue the point, but in truth, the fullness of the dynamic stillness of the one is the same as the profoundly blissful emptiness of the other. The point is to see that this individual life we have—our personal life and our physical existence—is profoundly uncertain because it is filled with ambiguity and pain. If we cannot deal with the uncertainty, ambiguity, pain, and suffering, then we cannot grow spiritually.

But when we do have a commitment to a life of spiritual growth, then we are endlessly sacrificing ourselves in every environment for the sake of becoming the most truly understanding human being we possibly can be. For this, we cannot be avaricious, megalomaniacal, and lustful, although we can have money, compete, and have relationships. It is the groveling after things that does not allow for spiritual growth.

It is easy to get caught up in the worldly aspects of our existence—in the basic human condition—and to lose track of what spiritual growth really is. It is not getting more of any thing. It is about finding in ourself and in this life, just as it is, an increasing joy, and in that joy, an increasing understanding of the infinitely clear source of all the diverse experiences that happen to us.

In America, so many people are struggling to get more,

and that struggle will eventually overwhelm them. For years, I have encouraged people to get the best education and to do as well as possible in their chosen endeavor. But in an authentic spiritual life, this emphasis must be seen for what it is—a training to be able skillfully to help others and to build an external confidence that reflects the internal strength we are about. This emphasis is not an excuse for external entanglement. Growing in a profession is not the same as growing spiritually.

The quality that we want to grow within us is that increasing experience of the power of spirit, and the only way this will happen is by trusting and depending on that power. We are not here to grow anything except an increasing experience of joy and an increasing dependence on the power of spirit within us, which is the essence of our individual life and of Life Itself. There is a unity to the whole of life, and our individual spirit is one with everything. Seeing that, we understand that what happens to us as an individual is not significant. We can see what an illusion it is to struggle with "I," what a waste of time to ask, "How can I get what I want?"

Spiritual growth requires commitment. We do not just

practice self-sacrifice until it hurts and then call it quits. What kind of commitment is that? No commitment at all. Doing something when it is hard is when it really counts.

Spiritual growth and self-sacrifice are interconnected. Surrender—trust in the power of spirit—is the key. Service is the more worldly expression, sacrifice is visceral. To provide many pounds of dates and thousands of almonds and flowers for a puja, which brings benefit to all, is a definite service. But the sacrifice is to burn ourselves up over and over again, and this burning is what allows for change and growth. When we are surrendered, we have given up our attachment and resistance—everything, anything. Surrender is beyond service and sacrifice and yet begins in each.

Service and sacrifice are not the same thing. Service is what we do for one another; sacrifice is what we go through when we are doing the service. Surrender is what gives the process the maximum benefit. If we are making some service because we want something back, it is not service at all; it is a business deal. In true service, we are making a connection and sharing, and in that sharing, we are absorbing, and there is a flow, an interchange, and through that interchange, a communion is established, and in that communion, there is a oneness that allows for the infinite power of being to manifest in the field of diversity. So true service is not about two or several; it is not about individual agendas.

Without self-sacrifice, there can be no surrender because we are always struggling to achieve something for ourselves. Sacrifice is about giving up our personal agendas to contact that spirit within us that has nothing to do with agendas. From the perspective of spirit, our struggles for personal agendas have no reality; spirit has no concern for anything we think we want. So why would we deny our contact with that total well-being that is at the core of what we are for the sake of a thing, an illusion? By offering ourselves to the highest Self within us—by sacrificing our selves to our Self—we can experience the joy and peace that are the essence of what we truly are.

We deepen our life to enrich our life. This is not a selfish act. It starts out as an act that is centered in our mind and sense of personal responsibility, and it is also founded on our individual effort. But if real enrichment is to take place, we take into consideration the well-being of every human being we relate to, and as we grow larger and larger, we are taking into consideration the well-being of every living being.

Before we can see ourself as an energy event—which is what we truly are—and not a physical body, we have to be a whole, integrated person, which means that all parts of ourselves are in contact with one another. We are composed. The tensions have fallen out of us, and we feel the flow within and around us. We experience the tide of it. In every environment, we feel this fluid energy event that we are, and we can flow and harmonize with it. Because we are integrated people with our own center, we do not get lost in all the fluidity; we can flow and change.

In following this fluidity and paying attention to it, we recognize the total unity of it in us and in everyone in the universe, and at that point, the power of spirit within us attains its own self-liberated, completely natural-to-itself state from which it has come in the first place. Spirit has attained this state even as our body still exists, and spirit demonstrates this self-liberation before our senses. But we cannot become integrated without having some sense of self-sacrifice; the universal awareness we have of our own unborn, totally natural highest self brings the obliteration of any notion of individuality at all.

What we are growing in all this is joy and our capacity to be a more compassionate, loving, caring, giving human being. The world may come after us as we have some success in cultivating joy and compassion. It is easy to be seduced by positive feedback, as we start to think about ways to get more and more of it. This is when we have to be careful. We are doing what we do to allow the power of spirit within us to unfold us, not to get something more—something useless and illusionary—from the world.

Being joyous and growing spiritually are not a denial of our uniqueness, our bad habits, or a judgment of them in any way. Spiritual growth is a call to contact with a dimension of our existence that transcends all notions of uniqueness or bad habits—they are irrelevant—so that we can be truly ourself. Growing brings about a life of trust in and dependence upon—not in any psychologically weak or inappropriate manner—the power of spirit within us. Then we stop thinking about what is not in our life and start thinking about how we can make a contribution to Life Itself.

WE ARE AN
ENERGY EVENT

◦〜〜〜◦

"We think of ourselves as things; we do not understand ourself

as a process. But we are alive...we are constantly exchanging

and flowing....we recognize this energy within ourself,

and...we appreciate that we are a small part of something

boundless. And the small part that we are is in no way

separate from that boundlessness."

TENSIONS ARE NOTHING BUT
compressed and suppressed energy, and once we have be-
gun to dissolve them, we start to recognize ourself not as a
physical event but as an energy event. In recognizing ourself as an energy event, we feel the interchange that exists
among people. Some of it is pleasant, some of it is not.

But constantly, there is interchange. Life is exchange.

In recognizing the energy event that we are and in becoming aware of the energy event that everybody is—and the constant exchange that is taking place—we see that we are a process, an energy transformation phenomenon, and we begin to appreciate more fully the flow that is constantly going on within, between, among, and around us. Then, we do not see ourself as a fixed event, and we stop trying to define who we are. We see and appreciate our own fluidity, and we develop within ourself the strength to be fluid and at the same time not to lose our center. Then, wherever we are, we are at ease within ourself and in harmony with the moment.

A key to understanding ourself as an energy event is commitment: We have to live from some commitments, primarily the commitment to grow. This commitment is not to a teacher or to an ideology—it is to ourself and the preciousness that exists within us. We are committed to growing that preciousness. But commitment by itself is just another box. And if we are fluid events, fluid phenomena, boxes cannot contain us. What makes a commitment rich, alive, vital, and expanding—passionate and joyful—is devotion.

What makes it possible for us to leap from seeing our-selves as a physical event, trying to nail down and define everything—being so proud of and fixated on developing our special, individual identities—into a living, fluid event is devotion. It is a bit scary to make the leap into the real-ity of being a process instead of being a thing. We think of ourselves as things; we do not understand ourself as a pro-cess. But we are alive, we are a process; we are constantly exchanging and flowing.

If we just have commitment, our egos are going to deny us access to the power of the fluidity, the flow that we are. But with devotion, we will be able to face uncertainty and make the leap into the awareness of ourself as a fluid event and to follow that flow, live from it, be that flow that we are. Following that flow and living that flow, we feel from ourself into every single human being and from every single human being into every single living being and from there into the entire atmosphere, which is what is truly alive. All living be-ings are nothing more than condensations of the Life that gives rise to the total environment, the total ecology.

Having that depth of awareness, that attunement, takes our devotion to yet another level. That is a level on which our concern for our individuality is obliterated, as we appreciate the dynamics and the difficulty that all living beings and the total environment face to recreate and re-express themselves continuously. In living in attunement to that difficulty, through devotion, we become profoundly compassionate.

Then, we have a center from which we move, but we no longer have any individuality we are seeking to satisfy or reinforce. Our awareness becomes an infinite awareness. It becomes spiritual liberation because our spirit, that energy event that we are, has reasserted itself in its own original nature—pure spirit—unbounded in any way by our mind, tensions, supposed limitations. We are liberated beings functioning for the benefit of all living beings. We understand that never are there two, there is only one. There is no other.

At that point, there is no need for answers because there are no questions. There is just endless, infinite, creative activity that is constantly serving to eliminate the suffering of all the individual events that exist within the whole. To fulfill the preciousness within each of us and to live from the experience of total well-being that is the essence of that preciousness take a commitment that matures into authentic devotion, and this is work. And that devotion, while always remaining one-pointed, becomes vast.

Energy lines exist among all of us and throughout the whole environment. Just as there are currents in the ocean and the air, so, too, within every dimension of the environment underlying all these currents are energy channels, energy systems. First, we recognize this energy within ourself, and as we feel it more and more, we appreciate that we are a small part of something boundless. And the small part that we are is in no way separate from that boundlessness. We are in no way isolated from it—there is no boundary or barrier between us and it. My own speculation is that there is only one nervous system on the planet. There is no up there or down there—there is only right here. Any limitation we have is purely a function of our imaginations. Because what is alive within us is in no way separate from the Life of the whole of the world and beyond.

DEATH OF
A LOVED ONE

"What is living in our life will change but does not go away. We have to open ourself and allow our understanding to expand....we need to let go and see what happens. How do we let go? We send love."

SOMEONE ASKED ME THE OTHER day what happens to our relationship with a person we have been close to after that person dies. Does the relationship continue in some way? The intense energy, the intense contacts and flows that exist in our life, will change, but none of it goes away. It goes on without our direct contact with it, in much the same way that there are light and sound frequencies with which we have no contact, everywhere in any space we occupy. These frequencies do, however, profoundly influence not only our environment but also our functioning.

For us to conceptualize the dynamic of death as our dearest friend who just died or our father who passed away—*any* person—is to deny these energies the opportunity for their transformation. We are holding them to a limited perspective. If we let go of the event and let the energy of it expand, it can become completely different.

What is living in our life will change but does not go away. We have to open ourself and allow our understanding to expand so that we benefit from any expansion of dynamics around us. If we are holding onto an old form, ideal, or feeling, then we are limiting that which we say we love and that which is trying to work for our benefit. So we need to let go and see what happens. How do we let go? We send love. We love whatever it is. We breathe into it and open our hearts and interact in a subtle way with it. I have never felt for one moment, since his passing in 1973, that my teacher, Rudi, was not present.

Someone once asked me how discrimination relates to Rudi's choice to get on the airplane the night of his passing; he knew his physical life would end on the journey.

~

The answer is that Rudi lived in a state of total openness; he was not calculating the probabilities when he got on the plane. He was continuing to do what he always did— pay attention to the flow and the change of state. I am sure he did not notice he had died; he probably did not notice his physical body dissolve under him.

Rudi went on the plane that night knowing full well what was in front of him. Reading the dictation he was giving as he was flying, it is clear. He went, it is hard to say, courageously, because for him, it required no courage. Certainly he went fearlessly, but that is beside the point, too, because the depth of his dedication—so many years of continuing to deepen both his practice and teaching and to grow as a spiritual human being at whatever cost was appropriate—that was his life. There was never any issue. Full of peace and sweetness, he went on the plane to face the total uncertainty that was in front of him. No one else died in the crash.

Why should any of us be attached to this physical body? We know from the outset that it is not made to last. This makes our cultural obsession with self-improvement, beauty, and youth a bit absurd. Who are we going to sue when we die? "Hey, wait a minute, I've got a right to be here!" This is a joke. We cling to something that was never ours; we did not earn it—it happened.

This body is an expression of something far more subtle than what it is. It is not *our* body, it is the body we are in. That does not make it ours. We do not have control over it, and even those people who are fastidiously concerned about health and well-being get tired, old, die.

The night of Rudi's passing, Rudi was following the energy. He was not following a concern for safety, for remaining physically intact. Rudi was about flow. He was not concerned about his physical body; he was concerned about the flow. And he was ready to follow it anywhere.

If our hearts are completely open all the time, full of so much love, as was Rudi's, how concerned are we about our physical bodies? When we appreciate that the Life in us is the Life around us—that there is only one Life and it is very, very big—how concerned are we for a small part of ourselves?

FEAR, TRANSCENDENCE, AND HEROES, LIKE US

~~~

"Being the hero of our own life requires one thing the classical hero would have found unthinkable—surrender—not to anything outside—because there is no other—but to the deepest part within, to the power of spirit, allowing that power to manifest and express whatever it wishes for us."

A VERY LONG TIME AGO, IN Nepal, in the foothills of the Western Himalayas, in south India and then in north India, some people wanted to understand the point of their existence. They may have had families and some property, but they wanted to know about ultimate reality. And so they moved from their family setting into the most frightening and impure place their culture recognized. They moved into the cremation ground.

Cremation grounds in India are scary even today. They are filthy, busy, smelly places, swarming with bizarre people and regular people doing bizarre things. The cremation grounds are filled with the most intense emotions, which actually permeate the air. So the common reaction, so long ago, to the people who moved into the cremation grounds was that they must be crazy to leave the safety of home for a place like that.

Maybe the person who made such a move was a soldier who had witnessed his comrades hacked to pieces, or maybe it was a father or a son who had seen his family annihilated by some brutality. Maybe he wondered, "What is this life that is so painful?" Maybe he thought, "There is no life left for me," and rather than waste time trying to be normal, acting like everything was okay, he went to the cremation ground, sat down, and waited for his turn to be burned. Who knows how much time passed.

For these people, the past was gone and the future, too. And so were limitations. For without a past or future, with the exception of completely free, what are we? Living without boundaries. What then is in our life? Nothing

～

but the power of spirit, the livingness of Life Itself.

Eventually, a tradition of cremation ground dwellers evolved. It does not exist today, although one still sees in India people who have similar physical attributes to those practitioners of ages past. They were called Kapalikas, after the skull-cup they carried. They took their food in the skull-cup bowl—they did not beg with this bowl but fed from what was left after the death rituals; this food was what was left for the dogs.

If we were to meet a Kapalika, they would not beg food from us. They would not say, "I'm hungry, give me something to eat." Instead they would say, "The rays are hungry. Feed them." They would be referring to the rays of Consciousness emanating from that particular point. It would be an impersonal identification of themselves—and the true one.

From this practice of living deeply and constantly in the midst of physical death, a totally integrated understanding of the unity of subject and object, us and them, individual and infinite awareness developed. Early practitioners discovered that "I" all the way out to "you" and back to "I" again is one integrated event; there are not two in ultimate reality, there is only one. The pendulum of our awareness moves, on the power of the breath of God, from "I" to "you" and back to "I" again, back and forth, back and forth. I do not say that the pendulum moves on "the power of breath" because it is not the power of our physical breath but the divine breath within us, which breathes us, whether we are fully aware of it or not.

Over time, the Kapalikas had an influence on the courts and ministerial families of Bengal and Kashmir, even though they had no interest in followers. To move to the cremation ground was to abandon all interaction in order to live in the field of authentic Life. But authentic Life does not differentiate between you and me, us and them, me and it, and in an authentic Life, there is no desire and no aversion. So the Kapalikas had no desire for and no aversion to the following that developed around them.

That others came to share their experience was not an issue. It was part of the phenomenon of the examination of their own authentic Life. By definition, a vision cannot be communicated to the fullest in words, and so the Kapalikas' power or perfection was transmitted firsthand to those who came to live in the cremation grounds with

~

them. This cremation ground lifestyle was thought of as unusual, but it was also viewed as fearless, heroic. This lifestyle had nothing to do with restrictions of any kind. Eating the "right" foods was not an issue—remember, in the cremation ground, anything at all might be eaten, even human flesh. Sex was not eschewed. Appropriate careers were not discussed. Social forms were absent. These considerations were irrelevant.

What was relevant was facing up to every kind of fear within an environment that supported no false notions of security, safety, and certainty. Living in the smell, taste, look, and feel of death every single moment of every single day, the Kapalikas were like the heroes of classical mythology doing battle with the most fantastical monsters. But the job of the Kapalikas was much harder. The real work of every person who wishes to transcend the pain of this world is to stand up within themselves and stare at what they are afraid of—which is usually themselves—and walk through it with an open heart. This, the Kapalikas did.

Heroic feats that require mainly the attributes of physical strength and endurance require just that—physical strength and endurance mustered for a cause that the times consider noble. But a subtler kind of heroism that transcends all time, place, and egotistical notions like "noble" is that which seeks to confront one's own fears and do it with complete love: that which seeks to see everything the world is—all the pain and violence, all the delicious flavors—and embrace it completely, understanding it as the natural manifestation of the power of spirit. Then, in the midst of that embrace, that subtle heroism transcends everything in order to reside in and from nothing but that power of spirit—which is all that is real. Doing this requires transcending the physical strength and endurance of the classical hero—it requires transcending, while still in a physical body, the physical self altogether. This is profoundly hard work.

Such a hero embraces the things they are afraid of and learns about real love, accepting all manner of circumstances and people they do not necessarily understand. Can we confront the insecurity and fear we have, not about the whole of cosmic existence but just about what is in our heart? That is the most compelling fear human beings have.

Being the hero of our own life requires one thing the classical hero would have found unthinkable—surrender—

not to anything outside—because there is no other—but to the deepest part within, to the power of spirit, allowing that power to manifest and express whatever it wishes for us. It takes courage, guts to open and surrender completely in the face of the pain that is often present in our life. It takes real courage to be a spiritual hero dedicated to surrendering the whole form, flow, and feel of one's life to the unfoldment of the power within, in the time, place, and manner it chooses.

It is a genuine, an honest endeavor to try to liberate the discussion of spirituality from the context of sin, renunciation, rules and regulations to an exploration of heroism, because it is in the context of heroism that we will understand—not intellectually but in actuality—what it is to live our life authentically. What is the authentic Life and how do we live it? The authentic life is not the easier way, the more comfortable way. The more comfortable things are, the more we lose our true Life and our contact with that which is authentically living within us. It is hard work, living authentically.

For me, the authentic spiritual Life is one in which we seek to be the hero of our own life. Any human being has the potential to become the hero of their own life. All limitations can be overcome, changed, and the wonderful thing about our nervous system is that it is resilient. Our nervous system can be changed based on our focus; it will change based on that to which we relate. As we begin to attune ourselves to the power of spirit within us, to this finer field of function available from within, our whole life will reorganize itself in relationship to that contact.

To aspire to be the hero of our own life is not easy or comfortable—it does not make us fit in—because it means abandoning that which society identifies as "normal." The normal life is not what we will have if we are looking to unfold the highest potential within us. This does not mean that we will live, literally, in the cremation grounds, but it does mean that we will live every single second authentically, which is as if we did live in those cremation grounds. The cremation ground is representative of the endpoint of all physical life, all mental and emotional striving, and that is the same as what the hero does in living within and from the power of spirit.

Ultimate reality is everchanging, and there is no thing we can cling to that is eternal. Our bodies are not eternal;

our individual identities are not eternal. Only the power of spirit is eternal, and that is a process, a constantly shifting process, with no worldly security or certainty in it. And yet it is an undifferentiated reality—everything has one source—and in this undifferentiated reality, there is nothing to fear because if we have within us the power that has created the whole universe, what is there to be afraid of? No struggling exists within the Self that is our source, our essence. There is only struggle in our physical selves, which have no authentic reality to them because we are in truth an everchanging process, not a thing.

So in order to be the hero of our own life, we need to understand that fear is simply resistance to change—a clinging—and that our mantra is not, "What's going to happen to me?" Our mantra, in each circumstance no matter how frightening or painful, is: "I wish to grow, I wish to grow, I wish to grow. No matter what, I wish to grow."

To be the hero of our own life means to be the best person we can be, to have within ourself a consuming passion for loving Life and living Life, to go beyond the bounds of societies and cultures, beyond the limits of most human beings' understanding. We have to want to change

~

the quality of our life. This is not an intellectual under-standing; it is not an easy thing to do.

For the men and women of ages past who went to the cremation ground, there was no going back to "normal." They had abandoned any worldly aspirations. They lived only to pursue the heroic Life within themselves. They were not concerned with the "rightness" and "wrongness" of this thing and that thing.

One of the great tales of heroism in spiritual literature is the *Bhagavad Gita*. It is about a prince, Arjuna, who eventually finds himself facing his own family in battle. His family members have betrayed him, but he still does not want to fight them. In fact, he breaks down and cries: He will not fight them. His advisor is Krishna, his chariot driver, who is a sage as well as a warrior. Krishna, as the driver, handles the conveyance, working in harmony with the archer, who is Arjuna. Krishna tells Arjuna that it is Arjuna's destiny to stand and fight, that Arjuna has been trained to be the hero of this moment and that he has to stand up to the moment. Krishna explains that Arjuna must trust the infinite creative power that has brought him to the moment. He has to trust the resource within himself.

~

The battle in the *Bhagavad Gita* is a metaphor for the struggle most people experience searching for the fulfillment of their desires. The story shows that life presents many unfortunate circumstances to everyone, and rather than falling down in a heap in front of those circumstances or resisting them, the person who pursues an authentic Life focuses on what is to be done and does it. Such a person does this from a state of complete surrender, with the awareness that whatever happens, it is the power of spirit unfolding itself from within as the manifestation of their entire life.

In the *Bhagavad Gita*, even the most extreme manifestation of conflict in life is celebrated as the vitality of the infinite manifesting itself in the field of awareness. In the *Bhagavad Gita*, Krishna does not tell Arjuna to run away, take sannyasa, shave his head, eat brown rice, stay away from relationships. Krishna tells Arjuna to be above comings and goings, to be immersed in the awareness of the infinite power of spirit from which all forms derive. In the process of telling Arjuna this, Krishna reveals Arjuna's own infinite form and capability to him. In seeing this, Arjuna becomes peaceful and intensely focused because he trusts Krishna, who is representative of the power of spirit within. Arjuna then goes forth without fear of what is going to happen to him.

Arjuna goes forward to participate in the flow, the unfoldment of the battle, which is nothing more than the unfoldment of Life, and he does this in order to relate to and live in harmony with the total uncertainty that is Life Itself. In doing this, he displays the qualities necessary for one who is the hero of his own life: intensity, great skill, extremely hard work, integrity of contact, devotion and total openness to the teacher, complete trust in the power of spirit within. With Krishna's help, Arjuna faces his battle with courage, with love in his heart and clarity in his mind.

The example of Arjuna shows us that whatever experience presents itself in the field of life, it is never about the field. It is never about the "other," which is an illusion because there never is any other. It is about us. It is about what it means to be compassionate, loving, and strong. Arjuna's example shows us that the only person we are ever a victim of is our small, illusionary self because the real question is our own laziness, lack of imagination, fear, all of which act like Saran Wrap cocooning us in tension.

Instead of accumulating any more tension, we have to find the power within us and feel it and feel it and feel it, until it is something that, without hesitation, we feel in every moment of our existence.

The ultimate act of heroism is to sacrifice our own ego and will to the Life process within us. It is to be real as people; we do not project a cultivated image of ourselves, and so we do not live a life limited by the illusion we are projecting. Being real may not get us what we want—all ego trips are built around the desires we have. But it is only by being truly ourself that we will speak from a truer place within us—not Biblical or cosmic, just truer. Then we find the power of spirit recreates us, teaches us from within ourself every single day. Transcendence is not about being somebody other than ourself. It is about being in touch with all the dimensions of what and who we are.

People come to a spiritual practice with the idea of striving for some kind of enlightenment that needs to be looked for beyond themselves. But in an undifferentiated reality, there is no striving that will make us different from what we are. The heroic life available to each of us is not about making a journey from here to there to discover a new,

～

undeveloped tract of land. It is not a journey to another place. It is, instead, the unending process of total participation in authentic Life. This participation consumes our ego and destroys our patterning.

In becoming the hero of our own life, we are free to participate in the capacity of Life to endlessly recreate Itself, and it is Life's recreative capacity that frees us from death. Not that we will not die, just that at that moment, death is not even an issue—it does not exist. Living in the cremation grounds, the Kapalikas understood this. Becoming the hero of our own life, pursuing an authentic Life, frees us from the issue of death to participate in the endless recreation of ourselves in an infinite and vast array of form. This is not religion. This is a lived-through experience. This is true understanding.

I choose to talk about this in terms of heroism instead of in terms of the spiritualism of the Trika tradition, or of any doctrine or religious form, because for the hero, for the person who is striving to establish themselves in a completely different dimension of experience, there are no rules to believe in, there are no gods to believe in, there are no devils to fear. There is only the power of spirit within us, inseparable from us—creation and creator in one. In becoming the hero of our own life, we believe in our capacity through introspection to come to an understanding of the proper action to take in order to unlock the next level of crystallization. This unlocking is what our Life process is about.

We have to want to grow—we have to want it viscerally. And that visceral wanting will bring us into a state that transcends desire, the state in which true heroism takes place. This was the state of the Kapalikas, this was the state of Arjuna, this is *our* state as heroes of our own life.

CHÖD:

THE RITUAL PRACTICE

OF SURRENDER AND

SELF-SACRIFICE

"Chöd is meant to enable the practitioners and all sentient beings to cut through desire, tension, want, hatred— whatever impedes compassion for the suffering of all living beings—in order to find that place within where everything is peace and joy."

*C*HÖD—PRONOUNCED "CHEU"; the "d" is silent—is an ancient cremation ground practice of Indian Buddhist origin. It is probably as old as Buddhism itself, which is now about 2500 years old. Chöd incorporates an encoding of Shaiva (circa 3rd century B.C.E.) imagery, mantras, and culture, as well as of Buddhist iconography. According to scholars, Chöd has never been an homogenous tradition, a school of practice; instead, it has lineages, traditions. One of the foremost practitioners of Chöd, Machig Labdrön (1062-1153 C.E.), tailored the practice of Chöd to the particular needs of her students, giving them different meditations that led to separate lineages.

In the Jigme Lingpa tradition, which will be the main focus of this discussion, the goddess Prajnaparamita is invoked. She is the form of wisdom of the enlightenment accomplished by the Buddha and is pictured as diaphanously white, luminescently beautiful. She holds a flower stem in one hand, a book blossoming in the crown of the flower at her shoulder; with the other hand, she makes a gesture of consciousness. While people who have some material advantage (and that would be just about anyone in America by these standards) make offerings for a Hindu havan, or the Trika Shaiva Para Puja, Chöd is a poor person's ritual. Nothing qualifies a person for Chöd except their total surrender deeply within themselves in order to sacrifice their very body, their complete self, for the sake of others. The word "chöd" means "cutting through," cutting through the tensions, doubts, fears, obstacles, and obscurations that deny sentient beings access to the joy within them.

Chöd is meant to be practiced by a sole practitioner, just after sunset, or between sunset and midnight, in scary places or public places: in cremation grounds at midnight, at crossroads, springs, at gathering places. It is usually practiced with a drum, bell, dorje, and fringed headband as the only accoutrements. The fringed, black headband is said to welcome demons, who otherwise would be put off by the bright light that shines from the forehead of a Chöd practitioner. An animal skin to sit on is also appropriate for Chöd, but not necessary. No object is absolutely necessary to this ritual. Chöd is practiced in scary or public places because scary places evoke fear for personal safety while public places evoke the fear of censure or embarrassment. This is to break forever within the practitioners the notion that safety and normalcy are things to which to aspire. Public humiliation of oneself—doing things in public that people will criticize—has been a consistent feature of Tantric sadhana, or spiritual discipline, through

~

the ages. Such activities bring humility, as well as creating some distance between the practitioners and the temptations that might seduce the practitioners into a more materialistic lifestyle.

The practitioners of Prajnaparamita, of Chöd, go into cremation grounds singly, alone, and after taking refuge in the Buddha or teacher, in the Dharma or teaching, and in the Sangha or community of spiritual practitioners, they pray for all beings and ask Padmasambhava, the being who helped to bring Buddhism to Tibet in the 8th century, to come to the site and bless their activities. They also invite all demons, ghosts, evil spirits, negative influences, any obstructions, to come forth and be present. In addition, they invoke their own lineage of gurus, inviting them and all positive, productive energies that fill the universe to witness and participate in the sacrifice.

What is it that a poor person has to offer in such a puja? Only their body. And why do that? So that every unsatisfied desire, disappointment, broken heart, confused mind—every unsatisfactory circumstance—can be released, cleared, filled, and in that fullness, instead of being a force for bitterness, become a force for the good. Chöd is meant to enable the practitioners and all sentient beings to cut through desire, tension, want, hatred—whatever impedes compassion for the suffering of all living beings—in order to find that place within where everything is peace and joy.

As long as we live in the dimension of life where everything is a competition for something, suffering is all there will be. Rather than struggling for resources like all other living creatures, the practitioners of Chöd just give it all away and merge into the infinite. They give themselves so completely, and with such joy, to the liberating of themselves and every sentient being from all tension and struggle that to drop dead on the spot, filled with nothing but the infinite space and vibrant potentiality that they are, would be to them a wonderful thing.

And so, in Chöd, after calling on the productive influences of lineage, gurus, various manifestations of different energies as well as on the demons and unproductive influences—all energies that come—the practitioners visualize a skull-cup into which their body is chopped up and deposited. In Tibet, cremation grounds were not places where people were burned but rather where bodies were chopped

up and stacked on a rock for vultures and jackals to eat.
There is not enough wood in Tibet to burn bodies, and so
Tibetans did "sky burial." One of the most important cen-
ters for this is outside Lhasa; it contains a rock almost as
big as a football field and in the shape of a boat, which
Tibetans say a spaceship dropped there.

In chopping up their body and offering it in the skull-
cup, Chöd practitioners no longer carry in their heart of
hearts what they think is wrong with themselves. Instead,
in their deepest heart of hearts, they breathe and let light
in, and do good. Then, all the demons and ghosts, all fears,
are recognized for what they are—shadows and nothing
else. So having chopped up the body and put it in a skull-
cup, which is visualized as big as the sky, certain mantras
are done to purify the poisons that exist in the body, and
as those mantras are repeated, the substance in the skull-
cup becomes frothy. The froth overflows and satisfies the
demons. Through this offering, the practitioners are as-
suaging people's tensions—their lust, greed, hatred, and
brutality to which their fears give rise. In Chöd, we are
offering our body to cleanse everything that is frightening, brutal, painful, disgusting, and despair-causing in the

~

world. Simultaneously, the sweetest, finest, pure part of ourself, our love and joy, we are offering for the same purpose; there is no duality. In Chöd, we are asking that the demons become enlightened and that the fully realized deities have compassion for the demons, for us, and for all sentient beings. In the clear light of enlightenment, the true nature of all is revealed, beginningless, endless.

After the substance made of the body cleanses karma and obscurations, it becomes nectar or bliss. This nectar is offered, through visualization, to Avalokiteshvara, the Bodhisattva of Compassion; to Prajnaparamita, who is infinite space; and to the various forms of esoteric deities and teachers; to the knowledge-holding deities; and to the various dakinis, feminine goddesses of agency, who do things. Male deities in Tibetan and Tantric Buddhism are considered to be knowledge-holding, while feminine deities are holders of power. The men are more pacific, the women more active.

In Chöd, the chant at one point evokes the beating of the wings of the vultures as they come to take the bodies away, just as they would during an actual sky burial. During the dance of Chöd (Chöd may be done twice in an evening; the dance usually accompanies Chöd the first time, just after sunset, and does not accompany it the second time, which occurs before midnight), vulture movements are evoked as the practitioner stamps out the poisons of lust, pride, delusion, envy, hatred. Yet while the vultures are eating the body of the practitioner and carrying it away, the practitioner of the Chöd dance is the one making the vulture movements and chanting the vulture cadence. The vultures are also symbolic of dakinis, from whom the practitioner frequently seeks help. In this way, offering and offerer are one; dualism is nonexistent. Negative and positive become indistinguishable.

Thus, we make our Chöd offering in the nicest way. We say, "Please, demons, accept my body, take a piece of me. Taking a piece of me, become satisfied, because there certainly is more than enough to go around, and when you are satisfied completely, do good work and help people. And in the process of doing good work and helping people, please seek enlightenment, seek Bodhichitta. In other words, take up a good path in your life."

As mentioned earlier, there is a tradition of Chöd where the practitioner does the ritual alone, albeit in a public place or cremation ground. There is also a group practice of Chöd in which a company of people is gathered to do the same offering, but in this case, the practitioner offers his or her body to the demons that inflict the people gathered there. The practitioner is offering him- or herself completely to those demonic diseases, anxieties, tensions, angers, hatreds for the sake of bringing about health and happiness in all the people with whom the practitioner associates. In other words, the practitioner takes on those demons, feeds and nurtures them, and sends them away in a nice way, with a compassionate impulse, to be of benefit to all sentient beings.

So Chöd is a total sacrifice of everything we think we have, including our flesh and blood, and everything we think we are, in order to pacify our tensions and those of other people at the same time that we are generating Bodhichitta, the awakened state of mind. In Chöd, we give away our body, our entire life, recognizing that people have desires but seeing those desires as demons; and this is because among all of us, but especially among poorer people, any desire is going to intensify the tremendous physical struggle into which sentient beings have been born. Thus, having satisfied the demons, we contemplate that part of

⁓

ourself that is beyond our body and mind. We contemplate that aspect of our existence that is infinitely spacious.

In this contemplation, we begin to understand that everything related to our mind has nothing to do with anything. As we begin to contemplate the infinitely spacious, pure potentiality that we are, we realize that there is no mind in that. There is no thought, no desire, no need. It is not that we have a dualistic fight with our mind; it is simply that our mind, as we are used to it functioning on a daily basis, has nothing to do with infinite spaciousness, with ultimate reality as beginningless and endless. That infinite spaciousness has no problem whatsoever. It is radiant, luminous, perfectly clear perfection that extends infinitely and unbroken.

The contemplation in Chöd of infinite space as the fundamental core of what we are is the highest dimension of contemplation that exists within Tantric practice. This is the part of us that is completely beyond desire, want, need, any issue at all. In infinite space, we have no physical body about which to be concerned. In infinite space, there is no "other" to discuss and no need. There is no mind that does the contemplating; ultimately, there is no

~

contemplator, no contemplating, no object. There is only infinite potentiality expressing from itself automatically, according to its own program, all the diversity of form and function that exists as the ordinary life of human beings, both individually and collectively.

There is an extraordinary scientific reality underlying this. A human being is nothing but a colony of cells, and the mind is a function of our physical body and not the reverse. The way in which individual colonies of cells interact with one another gives rise to the differences in human beings and is also the source of our similarity. These colonies of cells that we are, on a physical level, are why we desire relationships and things because these colonies have a biological mandate: to reproduce and to eat. So the thrust of our physical lives is survival, money, reproduction, the fulfillment of every kind of desire.

But there is something that animates these colonies of cells, and that something is beyond physical concerns. It vitalizes these colonies and makes them dynamic. And that vitality, that dynamic force, is what we are concerned about here.

Geneticists have widely accepted that all nucleated cells, which are the ones that make up animal, plant, and fungal bodies, are essentially the same. Nucleated cells subdivide in order to reproduce themselves, and they have evolved from symbiotic relationships between bacteria because at some point, one kind of bacteria tried to eat another kind of bacteria and could not digest it. So to put it simply, depending upon which kinds of bacteria combined with one another, plants, animals, humans, or fungi manifested.

What this means is that if it were not for grace, we might be cabbages. While we are more complex and sophisticated in terms of our structure and organization, there is no more intelligence invested in a human being than in any other life form. On this planet, all life manifested from one basic life form, and everything else is that life form's adaptation to different environments through combining itself in different ways, reorganizing itself in different ways—giving rise to structure.

This whole environment we live in is one. The air, water, sunlight, oceans, land, everything—it is all one thing, one living event. This planet is one living event. We are not the source of life on this planet; we are not the highest life on this planet. We are an effect; the body is an effect of the life that exists on this planet.

~~~

Through our spiritual practice—through practices such as Chöd—we are attempting to arrive at a palpable, concrete contact with the immeasurably vast and inconceivably ancient ultimate reality. The minerals that make up our bodies have landed here from unimaginable distances, planetary systems billions of light years away, and these elements that compose us have been many times used in many different forms of life. We have been many, many, many things, and we carry in us the vibration of many different life forms and life experiences. As people who wish to grow spiritually, we want to access the wisdom of all that experience, to allow us to find peace, understanding, and joy within ourself as the beginningless and endless dance of Consciousness, of which we are a part, unfolds.

Life Itself is making us, giving rise to us, dissolving us, giving rise to us again, dissolving us again—endlessly. To have this recognition is to put an end to our hopes, fears, issues because, having seen our lives from the highest ground, what is there to defend? What is there to seek? What is there to accumulate or acquire? There is only the capacity to tune into the music of life and feel it, to attune ourselves to it completely, to live in harmonious concert with this vibrancy, this vitality, as it expresses itself in the form of our life, whatever life that may be. Chöd is a spiritual practice that celebrates this.

Everybody has pain, suffering, tensions in their life. But a feeling of worthlessness, a sense of doubt about ourselves, this is inappropriate, illusory; we do not have to be afraid. The power that created the whole universe is in us. When we access it, we transcend self-doubts, doubt about life, and every kind of fear, and the joy we feel in the clarity within us obliterates any idea that we need something different or additional.

Chöd is the ancient underpinning of all ritual practice, and it speaks to the transcendence of all our doubts and fears in order to dwell in the infinite spaciousness that we are. In Chöd, we are cutting ourselves up and passing ourselves out so that every living being may discover and live from that infinite spaciousness within. This cutting ourselves up and passing ourselves out is what is really going on in life anyway; it is Rudi's "spiritual cannibalism," a process that is understood scientifically as symbiosis—the evolution of all life forms on the planet. There is a constant interchange because life is nothing

~

but rhythmic balanced interchange. Exchange is life; flow is exchange; flow is Life.

Life as exchange and interchange means that we are aware all the time of the circulation of energy constantly going on among us and the people in our environment and between us and the environment itself. That awareness intensifies our experience, and as we establish ourself in the highest place, a much more powerful event is allowed to unfold. The highest moral and ethical training is not, "Do this, don't do that." It is to feel into ourself, feel into another human being, feel the interchange, the flow, between the two and to be aware of what and how it is appropriate to serve that person. Chöd is a ritual act through which we perform that service and sacrifice, having first generated the surrender necessary to give ourselves away completely. Chöd is a ritual act through which we release ourselves—and allow for the possibility of the release of every sentient being—into the flow of the infinite.

Once the energy is established in a spot, flow happens. This is why the practitioner of Chöd first calls upon the energy of the teacher, teaching, community, and various dakinis and beings to come to the site of practice. Likewise, in meditation, we emphasize flow in the beginning because our physical body becomes naturally stronger and more able to practice from the awareness of the channels and circulation. In meditation, our body is the site in which we establish the energy, the flow. It is like giving ourselves an acupuncture treatment, intensifying the vitality of the circulation and channels. If we are aware of flow, we can begin to see how any energy extends itself through time and space. We can see what various combinations of energy will give rise to and how they will work out. This flow is a reciprocal interchange between body, mind, and infinite spirit, and being established in that infinite flow is khecari mudra.

Chöd, Phowa, the Para Puja of the Trika, Rudi's time and space work, and Nityananda's "sky of the heart" all have khecari mudra in common. Underlying the activity and visualization of Chöd, as well as of these other practices, is the practice of khecari, which means "moving in the firmament." This can be confused with discussions of astral travel, which it is not. Truthfully, there is no such thing as astral travel. For the person who has the capacity to experience fully khecari mudra, living in the experience

~

of oneself as a wave of potentiality existing in infinite space, who needs to travel—to where?

In khecari mudra, a person's vital energy is gathered up in the chakra below the navel, and after that energy is gathered up, it is brought from below the navel to the heart, where it is transformed into an experience of sweetness and joy, and from the heart to the head, commonly thought of as "between the eyebrows and above." There is a secret here because "between the eyebrows and above" is not exactly right. The real chakras begin in the palate, above the roof of the mouth. There are two chakras: one behind the sinuses and nose and another one slightly above that. So we bring the energy there but inside, not on the surface. Then, after that energy has become vibrant, it is projected out the top of the head, twelve finger-breadths above it— as far as we can possibly project it. This is khecari mudra; an open heart is essential to this. We have to take the time every day to sit and feel our heart chakra, and to let the energy work there, allowing the heart to open fully. Then the energy can easily rise up. This is important.

When Nityananda talks about sky of the heart, he is saying that the real heart of our spiritual practice is the opening of the chakra in our head and the rising up of this energy beyond our physical body to that point where we are connected to and contemplating the infinite space that has no mind. This is that state of the person, as in Chöd, who has surrendered everything—their body, everything. This is the person who lives in the state where their entire mechanism is open, connected to, and participating, as a wave of total potentiality, in complete concert with infinite space.

In Chöd, our appreciation of ourself as infinite spaciousness is manifested in the visualization in our navel of a red female—the red, naked dakini, Dorje Phagmo—standing on a golden disk. She is the vital force, the individual goddess who rises up within us. She forms in the belly, carrying the skull-cup and curved knife of the sky burial ground. Having taken form with the mantra "Phat"—said with the out-breath projected upward—she comes up from the navel chakra to the heart through the palate and out the top of the head. She transforms into the Black Goddess, the Tibetan form of the Indian goddess, Kalasamkarshini, and whacks off our head, takes our skull, makes a space without end, dumping our body in it—and boils us. Once the flesh is eaten, nothing more remains but our essence, which is the infinite space that we truly are, even with a physical body.

In the Saraswati order in India, the orange cloth worn by monks is intentionally the color of the stained shrouds of the dead in a cremation ground, because this is one way of saying that there is no longer a person here; this person has passed beyond individual identity. Rather, this is "ananda," bliss, a wave of potentiality moving in the firmament of infinite space. The sky of the heart is the inner sky—infinite space—that exists within us. The infinite dimensions of space cannot be contacted with the physical senses, only with the inner senses. For example, our ability to perceive light is limited; there is much more light on either end of the spectrum than our senses are able to register. Likewise, do we imagine that there is no life that exists and operates in any other frequency just because we exist and operate in our current frequency? That is like saying only one radio station exists on one band of frequency, AM for instance. This we know is nonsense.

Through the inner senses, we become aware of our umbilical connection to the infinite, to God. And this is not a God who capriciously judges anybody. It is a God who gives life to all Life and stirs the pot, so that all the disorganization and reorganization is ever going on.

Chöd is a training method, but it is not about rules because the ultimate reality of endless disorganization and reorganization, which Chöd reflects, is not about rules. Rules will kill love every time. People need guidance, but they do not need a list of dos and don'ts. Any rules that we have, the minute we move them into time and space, become obstructions. We have to be free, unbounded, able to unwind our trauma, tension, karma in any way that is appropriate to us. We have a living teacher so that we understand the appropriate way to practice and do not fall down in our effort, thereby creating more karma for ourselves. The teacher is our stillpoint, our frame of reference. Without the teacher, our mechanism cannot get powered up enough to crush the weight of trauma and pain that everybody brings to this world. And crushing this weight is necessary in order to bring the energy out. With the teacher, we need to be loving and trusting. This is an act of faith and is part of trusting the Life process. This way, our egos are destroyed, our tensions, unwound, and the love and joy in our heart are free to rise up.

Chöd and the Kaula puja are not about judging what is pure and impure. In the Para Puja, which is a Kaula puja, everything human beings can possibly find pleasurable is offered and is appropriate; in Chöd, whatever any demon wants is appropriate to give. So in the Para Puja, we give wine, meat, fish, our physical body. In Chöd, we rip out our veins, tear out our organs, feed everything to everybody. There is no judgment: "Oh, you're an inappropriate person to sit at my table. This is appropriate, that's inappropriate; this, pure, that, impure." We have no judgments about which demons will become our protectors. We just nourish everyone.

Our inner practice of these pujas, including Chöd with its Buddhist traditions, is kundalini yoga. The ultimate goddess of these pujas, whether Hindu or Buddhist, is infinite consciousness, infinite spaciousness and dynamism, contemplated as existing far beyond physical form. This practice puts us ever more deeply in touch with that aspect of our existence which is beyond every kind of temporal-spatial limitation, causing us to appreciate the vast potentiality inherent in our life.

To connect to that potential does not mean that we have some additional willpower. It means that there are some additional powers spontaneously operating within the field of our life which cannot be touched by our mind or our will. Pujas like Chöd acknowledge, cultivate, nourish the awareness of these powers. These powers with which we harmonize have the possibility to do good, in the sense that anything expansive of our awareness and of our sense of peace and joy is a wonderful, extraordinary thing. These energies bring about growth and free us from attachment; we cannot keep our energy above our head when we are constantly struggling with so many desires below.

To be completely connected in that place beyond time and space, we cannot cheat our tensions; we cannot cheat our karma. We can only be responsible for that karma, satisfy it, as we do the demons in Chöd, and get on with our life. People who want to negotiate with their karma end up endlessly attached to the treadmill of life.

We can only get over the suffering, cut through it, as in Chöd; we do not want to suppress it. We are not here to suppress anything because that would be suppressing the flow. That willful act of suppression is in fact the source of

~

endless repetition of karma. Jamming down, denying, trying to hide from ourselves, our mind, and our life—this is pain. Letting everything go in a somewhat disciplined environment—feeling and trusting the flow—gives us the chance to focus our energy so that our life force will be internalized, gathered, allowed to rise up and refine itself until our contact with the infiniteness of Life Itself makes possible our complete release from all the bindings that hold us in an unpleasant place.

The sacrifices of pujas such as Chöd and the Para Puja of the Trika tradition of Shaivism have at their core unburdening ourselves, getting rid of our weight, releasing our holding-on so that a flow can take place. Rudi used to say that every human being lives in a sheath about a foot thick. When we take our awareness beyond that sheath and dissolve the sheath, we have the possibility of experiencing the infiniteness that we are. We let go of every thing and any thing so that the flow of our vital force allows for khecari mudra, where our energy is fully unfolded and totally dissolved into the infiniteness of the sky of the heart.

Ordinarily a mudra is a posture intended to bring about a certain vibration in our body by sinking into the channels, bringing about a specific vibration in them. And the vibration of the channels brings out a certain quality within our awareness. Even though there is discussion in some texts of gestures for khecari mudra, this mudra is not actually a physical posture or gesture. It is an energetic posture wherein our energy is fully unfolded and totally dissolved into the infiniteness of the heart sky. Khecari mudra is holding ourself in the infinite, accessible completely from within us, and staying there as long as we can. When our energy has been gathered and brought from chakra to chakra, been opened beyond our head, outside our body, to that point twelve finger-breadths above our head, and then held there, expanding and expanding to become what we truly are—a vast wave of pure peace, of pure potentiality—this is khecari mudra.

The highest practice of the fulfillment of kundalini yoga and the achievement of ultimate enlightenment are attained when a person has the capacity to hold their energy in that state at all times. Achieving that requires a profound sacrifice of everything we hold onto; it means relinquishing every single thing, and I mean every single thing, to which we are attached, just as we do in the ritual practice of Chöd.

~

Hence, the encouragement to live simply. The more simply we live, the fewer attachments we have and the less overhead we generate, in which case, the fewer attachments we have to give up and the less pain and suffering.

Khecari mudra is the awakening of our own individual life force to bring it from chakra to chakra to the top of the head. Then the reciprocal interchange from this individual mechanism to that infinite spaciousness and back—the flow—is the source of the dissolution of all bonds that hold our elements together as an individual event. Having established ourself in that state and having existed there, the body will naturally, in due course of time, unwind its traumas, stresses, strains, pain, suffering, karma. The body will release its own personal history completely. As it releases its personal history, it will unwind all bindings that hold the elements together, and then forever and ever, this individual life is dissolved. All this individual karma, this mindstream, is joined with and completely emptied into the infinite stream that gives rise to all form and function. This is when we know that we are nothing but the breath of God.

Khecari mudra is the fulfillment of kundalini yoga, the

point of Chöd. We sacrifice everything we hold onto so that our energy, on its own, naturally rises up to that point of absolute maturity. This is the essence of Rudi's Tantric teaching, of Nityananda's life work, of Abhinavagupta's, and of Padmasambhava's. This teaching has been thought of historically as "secret"—the secret teaching—because without an authentic, living guru, a practitioner cannot realize the power of such practice. When the energy rises up an inch in a practitioner who does not have an authentic, living guru, it energizes ambitions, desires, tensions, confusions, wants, needs, and all egotistical issues. All these are fired up, and without a teacher, the person ends up falling on their face.

Thus, through a spiritual practice such as Chöd, we accomplish the awareness of the infinite clarity of that infinite inner space beyond mind—beyond concepts, judgments, agendas, fear, attachment. We understand that there is nothing more than joy to be experienced, and every form of experience that manifests in the field of our life, from that perspective, is something to be savored, whatever it is—joy and pain, happiness and sadness. To the practitioner of Chöd, happiness and sadness taste the

~

same. Everything is part of the banquet of abundant life that manifests in the field of pure awareness. Gems are beautiful and beach glass as well—and there is little distinction.

The real contract with God is that we give up everything we have and are, and God gives back to us in a richer way over and over again, endlessly. This is the point of pujas such as Chöd, of spiritual practices, energetic interchanges. It is Life Itself. Life should be about joy. When it is not, we do not have to leave the life we have, but we do have to change our relationship to it. Life is about joy; it is wonderful; it should be wonderful. We can make our own and each other's days a little lighter. And in this, God blesses us all.

A LIFE OF LOVE

"Love is when we care enough about a person that we let them be the way they are—in fact, help *them be the way they are. In doing this, all the tensions of their inability to accept themselves...can fall out of them.... We are...living a life of love."*

A LIFE OF LOVE DOES NOT HAVE any boundaries. A life of love is a life of uncertainty. When we love people, really love them, they are unique phenomena—unclassifiable, indefinable, totally transforming and transformable.

That is both a difficulty and a wonderful thing. It is difficult because human beings want to know. We want "it" to fit here in this place, and we want this to be there and that to be here. We want it all organized the way we want it to be instead of understanding that life has its own intrinsic organization that is sublime and sophisticated, subtle, elegant, and extraordinary in every way. We want life and people to be like we want them to be instead of learning to appreciate them the way they really are. When we love somebody, it is not appropriate for us to try to change them. Loving somebody and trying to change them are two different things. When we love somebody, we accept them as they are, and we have faith that if change is appropriate for them, love itself—the love inside them—will change them.

Divine love endlessly supports people and does not hold them back, does not cling or limit them, does not judge. It encourages us to make the best for each other that we can. Any authentic love is divine love. There is no other kind of love, when it is real love. There are hormonal chemicals that get passed around between people, but that is not love. Hormonal chemicals can go along with love, but real love encompasses much more. So we grow ourself and love grows with us.

Everybody thinks, "Oh, if I only had this, if I only had that." But right now we have everything we need because we have a power within that, if we connect to and live from it, immerses us in the state of—the feeling of—genuine love. This is a palpable point within us; it is a part of our mechanism, of our energy structure. There is a place we can feel, and in feeling it, we observe our issues, tensions, worries dissolve, and we see them for what they are— a function of resistance to things as they are.

Instead of thinking, "I need something different," let us take what we have and make it fun. Life actually is meant to be fun, and what blocks us from that fun is our obsession with needing yet another something to make us happy. Accomplishment is accumulation, and after we have accumulated all the things we want, we have to get rid of them, or life usually does it for us. Accumulation is the opposite of what we want to do; it is the opposite of flow and has nothing to do with real love. Ultimate love is to dissolve our identities and selves completely in a state beyond "me" and "mine," "I" and anything. It is beyond any kind of egotism.

Instead of expecting everybody in the world to become like us, we have to have enough love in our heart that we can begin to look at other people and see how they are and what they are, and do for them, even though it may be in a way that we do not instinctively appreciate. People in relationships often claim they love each other, and yet they struggle because each one is expecting, and even demanding, that the other one become like they want them to be.

Love is when we care enough about a person that we let them be the way they are—in fact, *help* them be the way they are. In doing this, all the tensions of their inability to accept themselves and the trauma of their deep insecurities of being unaccepted in the world can fall out of them. They do not have to act out anymore; *we* do not have to act out anymore. We are simply living a life of love. Then, the people we love can become what they truly are, and we can become what we truly are, because in authentic love, there is no "us" and "them"; there is no other. In authentic love, we understand that what happens for them, happens for us; what happens for us, happens for them. It is all one. In this world and beyond, there is only the infinite power of spirit manifesting itself in all forms, beginninglessly, endlessly—without beginning, without end—giving itself away over and over again in all the forms of Life, in a vast expression of complete, divine love.

A life of love is uncertain because the power of love will

bring up every kind of extraordinary circumstance that will be challenging. Our best ethical impulses, moral training, and greatest self-discipline will not be adequate to these challenges. The biggest challenge is inside us. That challenge is to find the love within ourself, to open ourself to that love, and to allow it to come forward every single day. It is a great challenge to allow that power of love to tear us apart and remake us a hundred thousand times—in the process, breaking our brain and exposing us to a dimension of reality profoundly humbling and awe-inspiring.

We have to take responsibility for our liberation. We have everything that is essential to that task right here and now, in the teacher, the teaching, and the community. The only reason some may not accomplish it is because they do not take responsibility for their mistakes; they do not become ever more skillful in the expression of love they are invoking from within themselves and living from every day.

This is a unique occasion, and we have the opportunity to absorb something special within ourselves. We can take this contact with specialness and use it to transform ourselves and our entire existence into a life of real love, an expression of real love. But it is up to us. If we each do not take responsibility and understand that it is our mistake, our misunderstanding when life becomes difficult and confusing, then who is going to change? If it is always that person's mistake over there, are we going to change? And if we are not going to change, then who is going to grow? That person over there may; but we probably will not.

A life of love, a life worth living, is not something we just find. It is something we build. We build it with hard work, dedication, with vision and the courage to take responsibility to live that life of love. The most important thing is that we take responsibility for the misunderstandings and mistakes that happen in every arena in our life and that we grow in the face of them. If we grow in a spirit of love and compassion for all living beings, our spiritual endeavor will not fail.

So we go forth trying to understand what love really is and to perfect the ability to express it in daily life. Love in the workplace, love in the home, love in spiritual practice, love in words, love in actions. True love is a total dedication, a total commitment, a total sacrifice. And at the same time, it is not a commitment that binds but one that releases, a dedication that is not a drudge but an in-spiration, a sacrifice in which whatever we give comes back to us in manifold growth. True love is something unbreak-able—it is infinite and transcendent of all tensions.

Our spiritual practice is not about transforming our-selves into something perfect. What we are doing is find-ing the perfection in what we are, and that is not in our emotions or in what we think—it is much deeper than that. It is in the power of spirit in all of us; it is in the power of true love, of divine love, that is who and what we truly are.

800.876.7798

rudra
press

www.rudrapress.com

Other Titles from Rudra Press

Will I Be the Hero of My Own Life?
SWAMI CHETANANANDA
Drawing on examples from the Bhagavad Gita, mystical poetry, and art, the author explores the criteria for becoming a hero. Although this journey may take you into the darkest places in your mind and force you to confront your deepest fears, it also promises the possibility of profound freedom and a life lived in the spirit of creativity, integration, and happiness. 200 pages, $14.95

The Open Moment: Reflections on the Spiritual Life
SWAMI CHETANANANDA
These eloquent passages direct the reader to experience the extraordinary power within-to a subtle flow of energy referred to as love, the Self, vital force, and God. Arranged into twelve central themes, this attractive book includes two-color text printing, gold ink stamping, and parchment endpapers. 120 pages, $16.00

The Breath of God
SWAMI CHETANANANDA
Refreshing answers to the questions and challenges one faces when undertaking a spiritual path. These essays are practical and inspiring-addressing stages in practice, mental disciplines, transcending fear and pain, and commitment to spiritual growth. 310 pages, $15.95

Songs from the Center of the Well
SWAMI CHETANANANDA
A collection of poems offering guidance on how to discover the transcendent within the ordinary. A book to refresh your outlook and provide an immediate, accessible sense of relief. 76 pages, $7.95

Choose to Be Happy
SWAMI CHETANANANDA
An attitude and a methodology that transforms your life into a continuously deepening experience of happiness. The author offers an alternative to the anxieties implicit in modern living. As he explains, happiness is not an external condition into which one stumbles—it is a conscious decision that must be made every day. The book includes an easy-to-follow meditation practice that will quiet your mind, help you develop calmness and sustain your spiritual practice as you move through your day. 230 pages, $14.95

Dynamic Stillness I: The Practice of Trika Yoga
SWAMI CHETANANANDA
This book guides you through the fundamental steps of building a spiritual practice: meditation, stilling the mind, releasing tensions, transforming psychological states, becoming a great student, and the importance of extending your personal boundaries. 263 pages, $15.95

Dynamic Stillness II: The Fulfillment of Trika Yoga
SWAMI CHETANANANDA
Here the author discusses the more advanced stages of spirituality: the strategy of effort, the energy of life, wisdom, facing death, and the awareness of the Self. 358 pages, $18.95

Open Heart Open Mind: Practical Lessons in Loving Your Life
SWAMI CHETANANANDA
These succinct essays speak powerfully about the paradox of love. This book explores the nature of authentic love and lucidly examines how to experience and live your life from a position of real strength. A counterintuitive approach to love which enables a person to let go, dissolve boundaries, transform negative patterns of relationships, release tensions, establish rapport, choose happiness, and open one's heart. 208 pages, $14.95

Spiritual Cannibalism
SWAMI RUDRANANDA
"The title attempts to put into perspective that Life must be consumed whole—with all its tensions, pain, and joy." With these words, Rudi introduces us to the concept of spirituality as work and describes his life of disciplined yoga practice and teaching. Rudi describes a series of techniques fundamental to an in-depth understanding of spirituality. 182 pages, $14.95

Entering Infinity
SWAMI RUDRANANDA
For Rudi, the foundation of spirituality is the wish to grow. As this wish matures, it evolves into a deep love of God and a love of life. From this deep love, one can surrender everything—form, matter, sound, all—and enter into an experience of infinity. 210 pages, $16.95

Also available: companion audiotape
60 minutes, $10.95

Rudi in His Own Words
SWAMI RUDRANANDA
This book provides a glimpse into the subtle spiritual state Rudi attained. In this book, he shows how to transform the energy in the tensions and stresses in your life directly into energy for spiritual growth and describes how to practice this transformation on a daily basis. 197 pages, $14.95

Rudi: 14 Years with My Teacher
JOHN MANN, PH.D.
Although the author was unaware when he crossed the threshold of Rudi's Oriental art store, he was about to meet his spiritual teacher. Set in Manhattan in the late sixties, this book chronicles the life of one spiritual student's awakening at the inception of America's discovery of Eastern thought and mysticism. 243 pages, $14.95

OTHER TITLES FROM RUDRA PRESS

Nityananda: In Divine Presence
SWAMI CHETANANANDA AND M.U. HATENGDI

While interest in the study of Eastern religion has never been stronger, few Americans are aware of the central position that Nityananda's teachings play in the understanding of Eastern philosophy. Who was this man who millions around the world consider to be one of the greatest saints of this century? What were his special gifts and insights that captivated their hearts and minds? Fascinating eyewitness stories and rare photographs offer an intimate portrait of the life and teachings of this Indian saint. (Formerly titled Nityananda: The Divine Presence.) 230 pages, $14.95

The Sky of the Heart: Jewels of Wisdom from Nityananda
SWAMI NITYANANDA
WITH AN INTRODUCTION BY SWAMI CHETANANANDA

An extraordinary book of universal appeal. Recorded in India during the 1920s, these verses contain the essence of Nityananda's spiritual wisdom. Because he spoke very little, this collection is a rare treasure of inspired words, spoken from an exceptional state of consciousness. Informative commentaries, a glossary, and rare photographs complete this remarkable volume.
340 pages, $14.95

rudra press

P.O. Box 13310
Portland, OR 97213-0310
toll-free 1.800.876.7798
phone/fax 503.236.9878
e-mail: rudra@rudrananda.org
www.rudrapress.com